The Development of Western Civilization

Narrative Essays in the History of Our Tradition from
Its Origins in Ancient Israel and Greece to the Present

Edited by Edward W. Fox

Professor of Modern European History
Cornell University

HEIRS OF THE ROMAN EMPIRE

By RICHARD E. SULLIVAN

Heirs of the
Roman Empire

~~~~~~~~~~~~~~~~~~~~~~~~~

RICHARD E. SULLIVAN

MICHIGAN STATE UNIVERSITY

*

Cornell University Press

ITHACA, NEW YORK

[c. 1960]

CORNELL UNIVERSITY PRESS

First published 1960
Fifth printing 1967

PRINTED IN THE UNITED STATES OF AMERICA

BY VAIL-BALLOU PRESS, INC.

Foreword

THE proposition that each generation must rewrite history is more widely quoted than practiced. In the field of college texts on western civilization, the conventional accounts have been revised, and sources and supplementary materials have been developed; but it is too long a time since the basic narrative has been rewritten to meet the rapidly changing needs of new college generations. In the mid-twentieth century such an account must be brief, well written, and based on unquestioned scholarship and must assume almost no previous historical knowledge on the part of the reader. It must provide a coherent analysis of the development of western civilization and its basic values. It must, in short, constitute a systematic introduction to the collective memory of that tradition which we are being asked to defend. This series of narrative essays was undertaken in an effort to provide such a text for an introductory history survey course and is being published in the present form in the belief that the requirements of that one course reflected a need that is coming to be widely recognized.

Now that the classic languages, the Bible, the great historical novels, even most non-American history, have dropped out of the normal college preparatory program, it is imperative that a text in the history of European civilization be fully self-explanatory. This means not only that it must begin at the beginning, with the origins of our civilization in ancient Israel and Greece, but that it must introduce every name or event that takes an integral place in the account and ruthlessly delete all others no matter how firmly imbedded in historical protocol. Only thus simplified and complete will the narrative present a sufficiently clear outline of those major trends and developments that have led from the beginning of our recorded time to the most pressing of our current problems. This simplification, however, need not involve intellectual dilution or evasion. On the contrary, it can effectively raise rather than lower the level of presentation. It is on this assumption that the present series has been based, and each contributor has been urged to write for a mature and literate audience. It is hoped, therefore, that the essays may also prove profitable and rewarding to readers outside the college classroom.

The plan of the first part of the series was to sketch, in related essays, the narrative of our history from its origins to the eve of the French Revolution; each was written by a recognized scholar and was designed to serve as the basic reading for one week in a semester course. The developments of the nineteenth and twentieth centuries will be covered in a succeeeding series which will provide the same quantity of reading material for each week of the second semester. This scale of presentation has been adopted in the conviction that any understanding of the central problem of the preservation of the integrity and dignity of the individual human being depends first on an examination of the origins of our tradition in the politics and philosophy of the ancient Greeks and the religion of the ancient Hebrews and then on a relatively more detailed knowledge of its recent development within our industrial urban society.

The decision to devote equal space to twenty-five centuries and to a century and a half was based on analogy with the human memory. Those events most remote tend to be remembered in least detail but often with a sense of clarity and perspective that is absent in more recent and more crowded recollections. If the roots of our tradition must be identified, their relation to the present must be carefully developed. The nearer the narrative approaches contemporary times, the more difficult and complicated this becomes. Recent experience must be worked over more carefully and in more detail if it is to contribute effectively to an understanding of the contemporary world.

It may be objected that the series attempts too much. The attempt is being made, however, on the assumption that any historical development should be susceptible of meaningful treatment on any scale and in the realization that a very large proportion of today's college students do not have more time to invest in this part of their education. The practical alternative appears to lie between some attempt to create a new brief account of the history of our tradition and the abandonment of any serious effort to communicate the essence of that tradition to all but a handful of our students. It is the conviction of everyone contributing to this series that the second alternative must not be accepted by default.

In a series covering such a vast sweep of time, few scholars would find themselves thoroughly at home in the fields covered by more than one or two of the essays. This means, in practice, that almost every essay should be written by a different author. In spite of apparent drawbacks, this procedure promises real advantages. Each contributor is in a position to set higher standards of accuracy and insight in an essay encompassing a major portion of the field of his life's work than could ordinarily be expected in surveys of some ten or twenty centuries. The inevitable discontinuity of style and interpretation could be modified by editorial co-ordination; but it was felt that some discontinuity was in itself desirable. No illusion is more easily acquired by the student in an elementary course, or is more prejudicial to the efficacy of such a course, than that a single smoothly articulated text represents the very substance of history itself. If the shift from author to author, week by week, raises difficulties for the beginning student, they are difficulties that will not so much impede his progress as contribute to his growth.

In this essay, *Heirs of the Roman Empire*, Mr. Richard E. Sullivan has reviewed the centuries of transition between the ancient and mediaeval worlds. The Carolingian period has long been recognized as the origin of Europe as we know it, but it has usually been treated by historians as a unique development independent of external influences. Mr. Sullivan has attempted to explain the critical changes which took place in Western Europe during these centuries in the context of the Roman-hellenistic world, in which not one but three new societies were taking shape, separately and yet in strangely similar and even interacting ways. Only against the dazzling background of Byzantium and Baghdad can the primitive simplicity or future promise of Charlemagne's court at Aachen be appreciated.

The unusual range of materials covered in this survey of three highly specialized fields has called for considerable consultation with other scholars. Both author and editor wish to express their gratitude to Mr. Deno J. Geanakoplos, Mr. R. Bayly Winder, and Mr. Karl F. Morrison for many helpful suggestions. They also wish to thank Mrs. Patricia Worlock for her editorial assistance.

E<small>DWARD</small> W<small>HITING</small> F<small>OX</small>

Ithaca, New York
June, 1960

Contents

HEIRS OF THE ROMAN EMPIRE

Introduction ～～～～～～～～～

IN 593 or 594 Pope Gregory I wrote the following lament on the state of the world:

What is there new, I ask, of delight in this world? Everywhere we observe strife; everywhere we hear groans. Cities are destroyed, fortresses are turned over, fields are depopulated, the land has returned to solitude. There is no farmer in the fields, nor hardly any inhabitants in the cities. The survivors, poor dregs of humanity, are daily crushed down without cessation. And yet the blows of divine justice have no end, because among the blows those guilty of evil acts are not corrected. Some are carried off to captivity, some are left limbless, some are killed. Again I ask, my brothers, what is there left of delight? If we love a world such as this, it is not because we love its joys, but its misfortunes. See what has befallen Rome, once mistress of the world. She is worn down by great sorrows, by the disappearance of her citizens, by the attacks of her enemies, by numerous ruins. Thus we see brought to fulfillment what the prophet [Ezekiel] long ago pronounced on the city of Samaria.

After making the proper allowance for Gregory's very human inclination to magnify the troubles of his own day, these few sentences provide an acute observation on the condition of the civilized world at the end of the sixth century and on the feelings of sensitive men toward the situation.

Gregory's warning to his readers to "see what [had] befallen Rome, once mistress of the world," points by implication to the existence of two conflicting trends disturbing society in his time. There were present in the Mediterranean basin institutions and ideas that had descended directly from the era of Rome's greatest power. These vestiges created in the minds of some of Gregory's contemporaries the illusion that Rome's civilization still persisted. But there were equally clear signs that something had "befallen" old Rome, that the remains of Roman civilization had lost much of their vitality amidst the play of new forces. An understanding of the history following Gregory's pontificate requires a grasp of the interplay of the old and the new.

One of the chief sixth-century vestiges of the older Roman civilization was the survival of Roman imperial government. In Gregory's time there still reigned one who called himself *imperator* and *augustus*. His capital was at Constantinople, the seat of the imperial government having been moved from Rome in 330 by Constantine, not as an admission of the dissolution of the Roman Empire but as a means of coping more adequately with its problems. Some of the emperor's far-flung territories had been invaded by Germanic tribes, but these successful forays of the barbarians in no way persuaded most of the inhabitants of the Roman world that Rome had "fallen." The barbarians, concentrated chiefly in the West, were incorporated into the empire as allies of the Roman government and in this capacity admitted the overlordship of the emperor at Constantinople. Just prior to Gregory's pontificate the Emperor Justinian (527–565) had repossessed some of the western provinces from their German rulers, demonstrating dramatically that Rome still lived on even if its center was on the Bosporus and even though some lands had been irretrievably lost to the barbarians. The emperors of the sixth century moreover continued to manage the affairs of state according to traditional political usages. They commanded the imperial legions in defense of the empire, deported themselves with all the pomp and ceremony clinging to their ancient office, and performed the numerous acts designed to assure the peace and prosperity of their subjects. The emperors still directed a well-organized bureaucracy, collected a considerable income, regulated the economic and social life of a large population, all of which combined to make the Roman emperor an important figure in the Mediterranean world.

Another apparent bond of unity joining the peoples of the Mediterranean basin was Christianity. After a long struggle, during which the followers of Christ adapted their faith to the needs of the Roman world, Christianity finally received the recognition of the Roman state early in the fourth century. By the end of that century it had become the state religion, and the Roman Empire had become a "Christian Roman Empire." In spite of bitter quarrels within the body Christian, the new religion provided a powerful unifying force in the Mediterranean world of the fourth, fifth, and sixth centuries; its dogma, ritual, and organization served as a common ground upon which men of different origins could and did meet.

Finally, there still persisted at the end of the sixth century a significant remnant of the cultural heritage of the Graeco-Roman past, another powerful force inducing men to think that the ancient world lived on. The literature, philosophy, art, and architecture of the classical period still played a vital role in the lives of educated men everywhere around the Mediterranean. Standards of excellence, style, and beauty were still measured by Graeco-Roman models. Especially important to the continued survival of that cultural heritage was the fact that the Christians found it necessary to appropriate pagan ideas to elucidate and buttress their theology. Even the rudest shock of the barbarian invasions could not overpower completely the cultural legacy of the classical past.

So it was possible and even partly justified for some of Gregory's contemporaries to believe that Roman civilization in its political, religious, and cultural aspects still survived to bring "delight in the world," to form the basis for a cultural entity encompassing the Mediterranean world. Yet Gregory's lament reflected the awesome fact that numerous afflictions gnawed at the remnants of Roman civilization, raising grave doubts in contemporary minds about Rome's ability to avoid complete and final destruction. Scholars disagree about the duration of the sickness besetting Roman civilization and about the exact moment of final crisis, but certainly there were strong indications that the situation was desperate at the end of the sixth century.

The political condition of the Roman Empire furnished cause for anxiety. Although the emperors reigning in Constantinople claimed authority over all the lands of the old empire and actually exercised it in some areas, their real power did not equal their claims. In the West several Germanic peoples were firmly entrenched in territories once part of the Roman Empire and ruled with almost total disregard for the claims of supremacy of the emperor in Constantinople: the Franks in Gaul and western Germany, the Visigoths in Spain, the Lombards in Italy, and the Anglo-Saxons in Britain. These Germanic masters seldom provided peaceful and stable government such as once had characterized the Roman imperial regime. When Gregory complained of destruction and misery, he was actually referring to the devastations caused in Italy by the Germanic Lombards, who after 568 challenged the Roman emperors for control of the peninsula. The disorder and conflict in the West must have raised serious doubts in the minds of any who still entertained the idea of the persistence of Roman civilization. As a consequence of the independence of the Germanic masters of the West it has become traditional in discussing the political history of the sixth century to speak of an "Eastern Roman Empire" rather than a "Roman Empire." Even in the East the imperial power was beset with formidable problems. The most serious was that of defense against the Persians, Slavs, and Avars. The imperial government encountered increasing difficulties in mustering money and manpower to meet these threats. For all its glorious tradition and exalted claims the Roman Empire in the sixth century was not the empire of old.

Nor was there anything like religious unity in spite of the fact that Christianity had become the religion of almost all the people of the Mediterranean basin. For in the generation of Gregory I the seamless garment of Christ was rent in many directions. Several important ecclesiastical officials contended for headship of the Christian body; among the most insistent claimants were the bishops of Rome, Constantinople, Alexandria, and Antioch, all of whom adopted some form of the title "patriarch" to indicate their exaltation over other bishops. The quarrels engendered by these claims, especially bitter between Rome and Constantinople, were often exacerbated by differences in ritual usage that set one group of Christians apart from others. But most divisive of all were the doctrinal disputes that raged in the Christian world. Chief among these was the long-standing disagreement over the exact nature of the Trinity and of Christ. This dispute originated in the fourth century and during succeeding generations had spawned numerous Christian sects. The emperors at Constantinople, claiming to be heads of the church and wishing to maintain unity, sought repeatedly to define a compromise position but only succeeded in creating greater dissension. The whole complex of organizational, ritualistic, and dogmatic divergencies set Christian against Christian and belied the contention that faith in Christ held men together in a common society of believers.

The much vaunted cultural unity was similarly turning from fact to fiction. The day when the ability to use both Latin and Greek with facility distinguished the educated man of the Mediterranean world had already passed. Gregory the Great could not speak Greek although he was certainly well educated by the standards of the West. And during the sixth century Greek began to replace Latin as the language of imperial administration in Constantinople, thus adding official sanction to a language barrier which already divided the intellectual life of the Mediterranean society. In the West the influence of barbarian Germans made it increasingly difficult to maintain ties with classical Latin culture. More and more the monasteries tended to become the only refuge where any semblance of literary and scholarly activity could be sustained. The monks, dedicated primarily to the service of God, were often highly selective in their views toward classical culture, tending to save only those things that seemed to them to promote piety. In the extreme eastern areas of the old Roman world, there was a resurgence of those particularistic cultural traditions of Egypt, Syria, and Persia which had made such notable contributions to what we now call Graeco-Roman culture, especially during the Hellenistic age which followed the career of Alexander the Great in the late fourth century B.C. For awhile, at least, when the Roman power was at its peak, these eastern influences seemed to blend into a cultural unity pervading the entire Mediterranean world. But the Near Eastern peoples never completely lost their identity nor wholly accepted the Graeco-Roman way of life. When internal stress and external pressure began to weaken the political fiber of the Roman Empire, the old traditions reasserted themselves, demonstrating that the previous cultural unity had been more apparent than real.

Gregory's lament therefore reflects a society at a crucial juncture in its history, a world caught up in a dramatic state of tension. The ancient tradition of political, religious, and cultural unity still persisted in the sixth century and induced in men the hope that substantial elements of the old order might continue to survive. Yet the obvious miseries of the age, some of them already centuries old, inevitably filled some men with despair. Many would have agreed with Gregory that afflictions so serious could only indicate that the hand of God was at work inexorably preparing the fall of the Samaria of Gregory's age—Rome. Hope and despair were the poles between which the minds of sensitive men in the sixth century were strung; and out of the situation created by such a state of mind was to emerge in the succeeding age a whole series of developments that released the tension by settling forever the fate of the classical world.

This essay will seek to identify the forces which ended the sixth-century illusion that the Graeco-Roman civilization still lived and which gave reality to the contemporaneous awareness of the dawn of a new age. Gregory the Great had no way of knowing what lay in store for the world disintegrating around him. But in the three centuries that followed his pontificate the Mediterranean basin saw three new unique societies replace the unified civilization of Rome. Each of them occupied part of the old Roman Empire and was akin in some degree to it, yet each extended territorially beyond Rome's boundaries and contained features unknown to the ancient world. These three new civilizations are usually designated as Western European, Byzantine, and Moslem. Probably few developments in world history are of more significance than the emergence of three civilizations from the matrix of a world at once old and new. The duality of their origin has left marks upon the modern world and makes of vital importance an understanding of the centuries in which new worlds rose from the ruins of Rome.

CHAPTER I

Successors to Roman Civilization

THE first phase of the history to be covered in this essay extends from about 600 to 750. During this period unity gave way to tripartition in the Mediterranean area, and one world became three. This era was marked first by the steady shrinkage of the Roman Empire and the consequent drastic internal transformation of that state. The changes were so overwhelming that some modern historians have felt it inaccurate to speak of a "Roman Empire" or even of an "Eastern Roman Empire" in the eighth century, and they have attempted to substitute the term "Byzantine Empire," derived from the name of the ancient Greek city of Byzantium, which Constantine chose as the site of his new capital and renamed Constantinople. The principal agents of this transformation were the Arab warriors who in the century following the death of their Prophet Mohammed in 632 conquered a huge empire stretching westward from their Arabian homeland across Africa to Spain and eastward to India and China. The Arab attack was not simply another barbarian invasion, such as those Rome had previously experienced. For the invaders were impelled by Islam, the new religion proclaimed by Mohammed. Islam supplied the creative element out of which arose a new civilization. Meanwhile Western Europe was stagnant and even retrogressive. Some of its Germanic rulers and a few of its spiritual and cultural leaders fought a losing battle against disorder and barbarism. With some justice this has been called the West's "Dark Age." However, even in the midst of darkness, the first feeble efforts were made to develop institutions and ideas suited to the situation in the West. In these efforts lay the genesis of a third civilization—Western European.

Transformation of the Eastern Roman Empire

The reign of Justinian I (527–565) is often cited as the turning point in the transition from an older "Roman" civilization to a newer "Byzantine" civilization. Actually the evidence relating to the period suggests that the conservative, backward-looking Justinian desired nothing less than to be accused of contributing to the decline of the old Roman order. His main efforts were directed toward restoration rather than innovation, and his reign marked a state of vigor within Roman society that had not been equalled since the fourth century.

His chief concern was with the recovery of territories seized from the Roman Empire by the Germanic invaders. Mustering all his financial, military, and diplomatic resources he directed his armies to a reconquest of North Africa from the Vandals, of Italy from the Ostrogoths, and a bit of Spain from the Visigoths, thus re-establishing direct control over rich areas that seemingly had slipped from Roman into German hands. Although Justinian's ambitions to reconquer all of Spain and Gaul were not achieved, he still ruled over a huge empire embracing North Africa, Egypt, Syria, Palestine, Asia Minor, the Greek peninsula, the Balkan peninsula south of the Danube, Italy, and a small part of Spain. Bureaucrats bearing ancient Roman titles and operating according to ancient Roman administrative techniques carried out imperial orders in these provinces. The great emperor held sway at his Sacred Palace in Constantinople, deporting himself with a ceremonial pomp and majesty that had been slowly increasing since the second century. His every wish was put into action by a corps of highly organized and specialized civil servants who populated the Sacred Palace. The emperor's officials collected taxes, recruited soldiers, directed economic life, conducted courts of justice, and maintained peace and order in a fashion much like that of emperors after the reforms of Diocletian (reigned A.D. 284–305). The codification of Roman law under Justinian was in large part an attempt to muster the past traditions of Rome, especially those deriving from the time that Christianity had been accepted as the state religion, to the service of a highly centralized, efficient government. Justinian—again after the fashion of most of his predecessors since Constantine—considered himself a Christian emperor as well as a Roman emperor. In discharging his religious responsibility he took all religious matters under surveillance, seeking to impose a uniform dogma on his subjects, to assure that qualified and reliable men occupied the great church offices, and to extirpate heresy or schism wherever it existed. Justinian's efforts to promote prosperity in trade, industry, and agriculture were successful. The emperor was as eager a patron of learning and art as were his predecessors; thus such monuments as the Christian university and the great cathedral of Hagia Sophia with its magnificent dome and gilded interior arose to adorn Constantinople and to glorify the imperial name. At the middle of the sixth century "New Rome" seemed hardly less extensive, rich, and well governed than "Old Rome" had been. Perhaps it governed a few less provinces;

perhaps there was lacking some of the ancient enthusiasm for Graeco-Roman civilization among the populace; perhaps Greek influences were stronger than previously. However, it was still Roman in essence and seemed destined to last for many years, given Justinian's success as a restorer.

Territorial Losses

Justinian's successors found that the great emperor's work of restitution had been ephemeral and even dangerous, since the resources spent reconquering Africa and Italy weakened the empire against more dangerous foes along its eastern and northern borders. For a century and a half after Justinian's reign his empire suffered one crushing military defeat after another.

The first grave crisis developed during the last half of the sixth century, when dangerous enemies struck from the west, north, and east. In 568, only three years after Justinian's death, the Germanic Lombards invaded Italy, seizing most of it except southern Italy, Sicily, and a belt extending diagonally across central Italy from Ravenna to Rome. The Lombards persisted in their attacks on the remaining Byzantine territory in Italy for two centuries. On the Danube frontier a new power, the Avars, began to create an empire about 580 and immediately menaced the imperial frontier. As the Avar danger grew, Slavic groups seeking to escape Avar overlordship filtered across the frontier and settled in the Balkans, weakening imperial control there. In the east the Persian Empire, bribed into peace during Justinian's reign, resumed its offensive. The imperial government increasingly concentrated its resources on this frontier but could not prevent the loss of Armenia, Syria, Palestine, and Egypt by the early seventh century.

The crisis of the first decades of the seventh century

was not entirely due to the vigor of the Lombard, Avar-Slav, and Persian assaults. Justinian's heavy demands on his subjects had created internal difficulties within the Eastern Roman Empire. His despotic government irked important elements of the population, especially the aristocrats, whose intrigues constantly impeded the efficient operation of the state. These intrigues were often abetted by dissident elements within the army. Especially pernicious was the incessant religious turmoil arising from the continued efforts of the emperors to dictate doctrinal unity. The emperors found that any doctrinal pronouncement alienated some segment of the imperial population. In general, the government followed a religious policy that estranged the Christians in the eastern areas of the empire —especially Egypt and Syria—and made them welcome foreigners who would liberate them from the religious yoke imposed by the emperor and his servant, the patriarch of Constantinople. Thus the blows which rained from all directions upon the empire which Justinian had so proudly "restored" only a half century earlier seriously shook its internal social, political, and religious order, and the beginning of the seventh century seemed to presage its speedy destruction.

With the accession of a great emperor, Heraclius (610–641), however, the empire discovered the strength to avert complete disaster. He and his successors managed to regroup imperial resources and to repulse the onslaughts of the invaders. Heraclius inaugurated the new defensive policy by his vigorous actions against the Persians and the Avars. Between 622 and 628 the imperial forces delivered a crushing defeat on the Persian forces and rewon the rich eastern provinces of Syria, Palestine, and Egypt, which had been overrun in the years from 611 to 619 while Heraclius

was restoring the army and administration. In the midst
of the Persian wars the Avars drove ever deeper into the
Balkans and attacked Constantinople itself, but they were
repulsed in 626, amidst stirring scenes of popular patriotism
and religious fervor, generated chiefly by the efforts of
the patriarch, who organized a constant round of night
vigils, processions, and sermons. They never again offered
a serious threat to the safety of the empire.

The struggle against the Avars and the Persians was but
a prelude to more desperate defensive battles waged by
the imperial government. About 634 the Arab followers
of the Prophet Mohammed began their first thrusts out of
their desert homeland. With amazing speed these fanatic
warriors wrested vital territories from the Eastern Roman
Empire and organized their conquests into a new state that
long remained a threat to its neighbors in the Mediterranean
area. Between 634 and 638 Syria and Palestine fell to the
Arabs in spite of the aging Heraclius' desperate military
efforts. The defeat was in part a consequence of the emperor's religious policy. The native populations had been
seriously disaffected by his efforts to find a doctrinal position that would reconcile eastern Monophysitism, the belief
that Christ had a single divine nature, with the view of
other Christians in the empire that Christ was both human
and divine. Many Christians in these areas preferred Arab
rule to dictation from Constantinople. When Heraclius
died in 641, the Arabs were already attacking Egypt, and
his successor, Constans II (641–668), could not prevent
the loss of that rich province. In the late 640's the Moslems
began to move westward across North Africa; by the end
of the century they had seized the imperial provinces in
Africa and were free to assault Europe through Spain. The
government at Constantinople, however, could hardly con-

tend with the Moslems so far afield, for they were also
beating at the very doors of Constantinople. While their
armies were advancing victoriously the Arabs began to develop sea power, thus launching a struggle for control of
the Mediterranean. Again the imperial forces found themselves on the defensive. Moslem sea power increased so
rapidly that during the reign of Constantine IV (668–685)
it effectively blockaded the sea approaches to Constantinople while Arab forces annually raided Asia Minor.
Finally in 678 Constantine IV succeeded in defeating the
Moslems besieging his capital and forced them to seek a
truce. A decisive factor in repulsing the Arab fleet was
the employment by the Byzantine forces of the dreaded
Greek fire, a chemical mixture which was hurled into the
midst of enemy naval formations by a special machine and
which burst into raging flames on contact with the water.
This defeat was one of the first suffered by the rampant
Arab armies.

The check imposed on the Moslems in 678, however,
gave little respite to the beleaguered empire, since a new
power was emerging in the north in the form of the Bulgar
kingdom. During the reign of Heraclius the pressure on
the northern frontier had been reduced by the defeat of
the Avars in 626. In the succeeding years many Slavs continued to settle in the Balkan peninsula, but they seldom
posed an immediate military threat. The case was different
with the Bulgars. This warlike Asian people settled at the
mouth of the Danube about 650, and at that time the emperors were happy to use them against the Avars. The
Bulgars, however, were soon at odds with Constantinople
and in 679 defeated Constantine IV, forcing him to cede
them territory and to recognize their state as a kingdom.
Continuing their attacks against imperial territory in suc-

ceeding years, the Bulgars, who had increased their power by incorporating Slavs into their kingdom, posed a constant danger to Constantinople and all but crushed the sorely tried emperors by this added burden of defense.

The Arab threat to the empire became grave again early in the eighth century. The Moslems were now in the full tide of their military strength and were making their supreme bid to dominate the whole civilized world. Imperial strength was at a low ebb as a result of the overthrow of the Heraclian dynasty and the succession of a series of weak rulers. Capitalizing on this situation Arab armies and naval forces renewed their assault on Constantinople, having virtually occupied Asia Minor and even crossed into Europe.

Again a savior appeared, this time in the person of Leo, a military commander of Syrian origin who spoke Arabic and who is usually called "the Isaurian" to emphasize his eastern origin. Leo III (717–741) seized power in 717 at a moment when Constantinople, under siege, seemed about to fall. Through his skilled and determined leadership the capital was saved in 718, and in the succeeding years the Arabs were driven out of Asia Minor. By dividing many large estates in the liberated territories into small farms to support free peasants from whom soldiers could be recruited, Leo provided for an adequate defense against the Arab danger for many years. Toward the middle of the eighth century the Moslem world experienced internal troubles that culminated in a change of dynasties in 750 and a cessation of the rapid rhythm of Moslem expansion. Not until the eleventh century did the Turkish Moslems mount a vigorous offensive that again threatened the very existence of the Byzantine Empire.

By mid-eighth century the subjects of the empire could breathe considerably easier: the Eastern Roman Empire had been saved from the assaults of Lombards, Avars, Persians, Slavs, Arabs, and Bulgars. But their joy was tempered by the sobering fact that the empire had been drastically reduced in size and changed in ethnic composition during the preceding years. Syria, Palestine, Egypt, North Africa, most of Italy, and part of the Balkan peninsula had been lost. Whereas the empire of Justinian I had been composed of many racial and cultural elements, the reduced empire of the eighth century was basically Greek in language and cultural orientation. This change in size and composition is in itself justification for saying that a "new" empire, chiefly Greek, had replaced the old. The term "Byzantine Empire" is usually substituted for "Eastern Roman Empire" to denote this change.

Internal Reorganization

The rulers between Heraclius and Leo III (that is, between 610 and 741) further promoted the transformation of the empire by revolutionary efforts to organize the available resources of defense. Their efforts led to the militarization of Byzantine society. The imperial government had for a long time depended upon mercenary troops, imposing upon the state the double burden of finding competent troops and of collecting adequate income to pay them. The constant wars of the seventh and eighth centuries, resulting in the loss of valuable provinces and income, forced the emperors to find a new source of military strength. Their solution consisted of placing the military burden on a free peasantry. They accomplished this end by granting to certain peasants agricultural holdings in exchange for military service. The usual practice was to settle soldier-farmers along a threatened frontier, assuring their services where needed. The soldier-farmers quickly became the backbone of the empire. The new system was used especially along the eastern frontier, thus increasing the role of the population of eastern Asia Minor in imperial history.

In order to utilize the new soldiery to the fullest extent, the emperors carried out a reorganization of the governmental system in the provinces. The old provincial system involving a complex set of military and civil officials was simplified by giving a military commander, called strategos, full military and civil powers over a specified area, called a theme. Each powerful general, dealing directly with the soldier-peasants in his district, became a formidable bulwark against foreign invaders who threatened his particular theme. The system far excelled in efficiency the older system of mercenaries. The subordination of the civil bureaucracy to the generals permitted the efficient direction of the total resources of the state toward the immediate military necessity.

The military and administrative reforms associated with the institution of the theme organization placed the peasantry in a vital position in the Byzantine state. The emperors took strong steps to protect the free peasantry, to assure their service to the state, and to curb efforts by aristocratic landowners to exploit them. Their legislation in this direction marks one of the most constructive phases of imperial policy in this era. The reforms checked an earlier tendency for the peasantry to become serfs laboring at the mercy of the landlords, thus creating a significant contrast with the fate of the peasantry in Western Europe in the early Middle Ages. And the reconstitution of the social order in favor of a vigorous peasantry had the total effect of increasing the authority of the central government in its relations with the aristocracy.

Religious Changes

The seventh and early eighth centuries witnessed significant transformations in the religious life of the Byzantine Empire, these changes tending to accentuate the separateness of that branch of Christianity which was centered at Constantinople. Perhaps the most obvious trend was the increasing control of religion exercised by the emperor. This, of course, was not a new development, since all late Roman emperors often acted as both Caesar and Pope, combining with their actions as secular rulers a close regulation of religious life, control of the clergy, and intervention in disputes over dogma. However, during the seventh and eighth centuries, the emperors supervised the church more and more. In part their success was due to the willingness of Greek clergymen to exalt the emperor as leader against the infidel Persians, Arabs, Slavs, and Bulgars. Heraclius, for instance, was able to arouse a crusading fervor in his wars against the Persians by playing up the fact that he intended to recover the True Cross, which the Persians had stolen from Jerusalem when they captured the Holy City in 614. The emperor's control over religious life was also strengthened by the final resolution of the long dogmatic dispute over the nature of Christ. This quarrel had repeatedly weakened the religious power of the emperors by forcing them to try to compromise with several dissident elements, compromises which repeatedly provoked wild riots in Constantinople and other imperial cities and which incited factions of clergymen, civil officials, and soldiers to defy imperial authority. The ultimate solution to this problem was possible only after the eastern provinces had been captured by the Arabs. Once these provinces, long so bitterly opposed to direction from Constantinople, were lost, the emperors could dictate a definition of the nature of Christ acceptable to the Christians remaining under imperial control. This was achieved by Constantine IV at the Sixth Ecumenical Council of Constantinople in 680, which commanded all believers to accept the doctrine that Christ's nature was both human and divine. Few imperial subjects quarreled with this definition of the true dogma, and the religious role of the emperors was consequently exalted.

However, that the imperial dictation of religious policy was not as complete as the emperors might have wished can be illustrated by the bitter quarrel over iconoclasm that developed only a few years after the resolution of the Christological dispute. The complex issues of the iconoclastic struggle will be examined in detail later. At this point it is sufficient to say that the quarrel began in 726 when Leo III ordered that his subjects cease using all icons in religious services. Leo's decrees were greeted with a storm of protest from clergymen and laymen, and although he resorted to forceful means to gain his end, he was unable to beat down the opposition. For a century after his reign the iconoclastic quarrel sundered Byzantine society, a reminder that the emperor could not always enforce his claims to dictate religious policy.

The generally successful, if increasingly autocratic, efforts of the Heraclian and Isaurian emperors to control religious policy had the further important effect of alienating the bishop of Rome, who was emerging as the spokesman of the Christians of Western Europe. From the pontificate of Gregory the Great (590–604) until the middle of the eighth century there was almost constant strife between emperor and papacy. During this era, as Rome was still politically a part of the Byzantine Empire, the popes looked to Constantinople for protection against the assaults of the Lombards. The Byzantine emperors attempted to capitalize on this dependence by compelling the popes to sanction their dogmatic pronouncements and to accept the spiritual overlordship of the patriarch of Constantinople. The conflict between Rome and Constantinople reached a climax at the middle of the seventh century, when the emperors were trying desperately to resolve the Christological question, and again in the early eighth century, when the iconoclastic question arose. To avoid accepting dictation from the East the papacy sought to rally the Christians of the west to its cause and thus to achieve a greater degree of independence. Although progress toward papal independence was slow and faltering, it was sufficient to open the way for the ultimate schism between eastern and western Christians.

The emergence of a Byzantine church, controlled by the emperor and confined geographically to the Balkan peninsula, Asia Minor, southern Italy, and Sicily, was certainly of great importance. Coinciding with the territorial constriction of the empire, with the militarization of the social order, with the de-Romanization of the population, and with the social and economic readjustment accompanying the military reforms, this development accentuated the uniqueness of the new Byzantine civilization, which was replacing the more universal civilization that had centered in Constantinople in the final stages of Roman history.

The Birth of Moslem Civilization

Probably the chief force effecting the transmutation of the Eastern Roman Empire into the Byzantine Empire was the shattering attack inflicted by a new power emerging out of the Arabian desert. The Arab victories of the seventh and early eighth centuries represented the birth of a dynamic, enduring civilization destined to affect the history of the Mediterranean basin in a fundamental way. For the Arabs, originating as unorganized desert warriors, rapidly developed into a powerful community united by the well-articulated doctrines and moral precepts of the new religion of Islam.[1] The birth of this religion and its impact on the Arabs were therefore central events of the seventh century.

Arabia before Mohammed

The Arabian desert and its population present a confused picture at the moment when Islam emerged. The bulk of the inhabitants of this impoverished land consisted of semibarbaric nomads organized into warring clans, each of which jealously guarded its flocks, its customs, its gods, and its proud independence. Life among the tribes was painfully simple and poor when contrasted with the luxuriant civilizations of Rome and Persia flourishing beyond the frontiers of the desert. There seemed no force capable of overcoming the separatism, the clannishness, the backwardness of the desert dwellers. However, the nomadic way of life was not the only mode of existence in the peninsula. Around its fringes played the political, economic, religious, and cultural influences of Rome and

[1] The Arabic word "Islam" means submission to God and is used to designate the religion centering around the worship of God as taught by Mohammed and canonized in the Koran. The Arabic word for God is "Allah." One who submits is called a Moslem. Moslems do not care to have their religion called "Mohammedanism," since this implies that they worship Mohammed the Prophet and consider him divine; this idea is foreign to Islam.

Persia initiating new developments and producing new tensions.

It was at Mecca, the chief meeting place of the desert dwellers and the outside world, that the new religion of the Arabs was born. Mecca was the seat of a sedentary clan which, as was customary among the Arabs, was governed by the tribal elders. But Mecca was also an important trading center through which merchants passed leaving both products and ideas. Through the development of trade and the introduction of foreign refinements, the way of life of the Arab residents of Mecca was gradually differentiated from that of the desert nomads. At the same time Mecca became one of the major religious, even more than commercial, centers for the nomads, for at Mecca was located the famous Kaaba, a small temple housing the black stone which the Arabs believed had fallen from heaven as a sign of divine favor. The sacred enclosure where the Kaaba was located also contained many other objects pertaining to the gods worshiped by the desert tribes. Many tribes made annual pilgrimages to Mecca to render homage to their gods; but the Arabs were also attracted by the wares of the merchants who lived there or passed through. The rulers of Mecca bent every effort to encourage the centralization of Arab life in their city. Thus the complex life of Mecca generated forces of great significance—the seductive attractions, material and cultural, of foreign civilizations, the political appeal of a possible Meccan hegemony over the nomads, and the compulsive pull of common religious worship. It was the coalescence of these forces ignited by the Arabians' driving urge to transcend desert barbarism that suddenly catapulted them on to the stage of Mediterranean history as major actors.

Mohammed the Prophet

It was Mohammed, citizen of Mecca and prophet, who unleashed the Arabs. Born about 570, into a minor branch of the ruling clan of Mecca, he was orphaned at an early age and raised by relatives who directed him into a career in trade. Eventually marrying a rich widow by whom he was employed, he was assured of wealth, not to mention prestige, in the society of Mecca. Yet, since he seems to have been introspective, contemplative, and ascetic, these worldly successes may have been of small importance to Mohammed. Beyond all doubt or question he found his solace and his destiny in religion.

An impenetrable cloud of legend cuts us off from Mohammed's early religious evolution. Perhaps foreign religions, such as Judaism, Christianity, or Zoroastrianism, all known in Mecca, discredited in his eyes the local Arabian beliefs and superstitions. Many scholars have insisted that Mohammed's ultimate religious pronouncements consist of a skillful synthesis of foreign ideas selected to fit the needs of his fellow Arabs. To the followers of Mohammed, needless to say, this conclusion is sheer blasphemy. They believe, instead, that Mohammed received directly from the angel Gabriel the full content of the new religion along with the revelation that he had been designated as God's spokesman here on earth. The first revelations occurred when Mohammed was about forty and from that moment he knew himself to be the Prophet, divinely ordained to utter the words of God and to convert his fellow men to the true faith.

Mohammed's announcement of his new mission was not well received in Mecca. His early revelations stressed a personal religion centered on the obligation to worship only the one God, and included the description of a last judgment where all men would receive reward or punishment, thereby indicating the urgent need for moral regeneration. For a people as individualistic as the Meccans all this held small appeal. Further his assault on polytheism was resented, particularly by those in Mecca who profited greatly from the annual pilgrimage of the desert tribes to the shrines of the old gods at Mecca. Opposition and indifference seemed about to doom the Prophet to failure.

After preaching to his unresponsive fellow townsmen for more than a decade, Mohammed decided to leave iniquitous Mecca for its rival Yathrib, whose residents showed an interest in his teaching and invited him to come and act as arbiter to pacify their quarreling factions. His emigration or Hegira to Yathrib occurred in 622 and caused the city to be renamed Medina or city of the Prophet. The Hegira proved to be a turning point in Moslem history, for thereafter Mohammed was the head of a state—albeit a very small one at first. His revelations took on a new complexion. Increasingly, they dealt with political decisions rather than abstract religious concepts. The simple preacher calling for personal conversions was transformed into the leader of a disciplined community of those faithful to God. Because they were set apart from the rest of the world by their submission to God, the community of followers of the Prophet was known as Islam. Increasingly Mohammed stressed the obligation of his followers to wage holy war against the nonbelievers for the glorification of God. On one occasion God spoke to Mohammed in this fashion: "Oh! Prophet, arouse the believers to combat. Twenty resolute men of faith will strike fear in two hundred infidels; a hundred of them will put a thousand of the faithless to flight." This sense of mission, coupled with the habit of warfare already characteristic of the Arab way of life, supplied the spark for the militancy of the new community. With this organized force at his command Mohammed turned against his former tormenters and in 630 was able to make a triumphal entry into Mecca where he destroyed the false idols and introduced the worship of the one God. The way of righteousness seemed justified to the faithful by this victory. Many Arab tribes, including the chief leaders in Mecca, some perhaps converted by the Prophet's religious teachings but others more likely impressed by Mohammed's demonstrated prowess as a victorious chieftain, hastened to join the community of the faithful. When Mohammed died in 632, he was the leader of a large confederation of Arab tribes whose union was built on acceptance of a strong leader and on a common religion. Having at last overcome their traditional disunity, the Arabs prepared to confront the outside world.

The Religion of Islam

Islam is a complex religion that has grown and developed for centuries; yet, like other great religions, its real vitality stems from certain basic beliefs and practices which date from its early history. Thus, at Mohammed's death his followers already adhered to well-defined beliefs and practices which held the key to the wide appeal of the new religion.

Perhaps the best definition of the essence of Islam is contained in these words from the Koran, the sacred book of Islam: "O ye who believe, believe in God and His Apostle and the Book which He has sent down to His Apostle and Scripture which He has sent down formerly. Whosoever denieth God and His angels and His Books and His

Apostles and the Last Day hath strayed far from the Truth."
Uncompromising monotheism is the central point in this
simple creed; the association of partners with God was the
most serious of all sins. A large portion of Mohammed's
pronouncements were devoted to a description of God's
attributes, and, although they were many, God was above
all a majestic, omnipotent deity, so far removed from the
human scene that man could only submit to His might.
God had revealed Himself to men by speaking through
angels to a series of prophets. Among the many "sent down
formerly" were most of the Hebrew prophets and Christ,
all counted as spokesmen of God. But the last and greatest
was Mohammed. The earlier vessels of God's word had
received only part of the truth, and their followers, by
accident or intent, had "lost" the original word. The religion of Mohammed, moreover, was all-embracing. God's
final revelation was intended not only for Arabs and those
Jews and Christians who had previously received some
part of divine truth, but for all men. For this reason it
was written down in "the Book" or the Koran, every letter
of which was binding on the faithful Moslem. Compiled
shortly after Mohammed's death, the Koran was the record
of the revelations he had received from God. Among these,
one fundamental doctrine gave peculiar substance and character to the new religion—the reality of the day of judgment when the good would be rewarded and the sinful
damned. By spelling out in vivid detail the joys awaiting
the blessed and the tortures in store for the wicked, Mohammed imposed upon his followers an overwhelming
sense of the urgency of religious obedience and moral
righteousness. Even though these early articles of faith
were expanded after Mohammed's death by the acceptance
of a large body of *hadiths* or sayings of the Prophet, Islam

tended to remain a simple faith which subjected man directly to the will of almighty God and which provided divine directions for human conduct in an inspired book.

Mohammed also prescribed a simple set of religious practices to be followed by the faithful. Every Moslem had to pronounce a simple statement of faith: "There is no god but the one God, and Mohammed is His prophet." Five times a day a Moslem prayed in a prescribed fashion. Such prayer was a private affair. However, public prayer did develop in Mohammed's time, especially on Friday. For this purpose mosques were built, where the faithful gathered and followed a prayer leader, or imam, in rendering homage to God. Here the imam often preached a didactic sermon following the prayers. Other obligations of the Moslem were giving of his wealth to support the poor, fasting during a holy season as an expiatory act, and making a pilgrimage to Mecca once in his lifetime, if possible. These simple requirements made unnecessary the development of a highly organized clergy and a vast church organization. Among the Moslems, worship tended to remain a personal affair motivated by the piety of the individual.

Since the faithful could merit eternal life only if they were morally pleasing in the sight of God, Mohammed laid down the basic principles for a detailed and extensive moral code. The content of these regulations is too extensive to outline here, but in general it placed an exacting burden on the faithful. Rigid dietary laws enjoined all Moslems to refrain from certain foods and intoxicants. Gambling, perjury, and numerous acts of violence were condemned. Marriage customs were carefully defined with a view toward limiting and regulating the Arabian practice of polygamy. Slavery was sanctioned but with strict controls. The Moslem moral law imposed much stricter rules of conduct on the Arabs than those to which they had been accustomed before Mohammed. In their puritanical tone many of Mohammed's laws resemble those of the Hebrew Bible. They impose on the faithful the same kind of obligation to practice sobriety, constraint, simplicity of life, and restriction of sensual gratification. The strong moral tone of the Moslem religion has always been one of its most attractive features.

With the establishment of Islam the world gained its third monotheistic, revealed religion. The three—Judaism, Christianity, and Islam—are the only such major religions. They are all intricately related by virtue of their historical descent. Judaism was the earliest one established. Christianity was introduced as a fulfillment of the Judaic revelation and absorbed into its teachings and practices many aspects of Judaism. Islam was proclaimed as a perfection of Christian revelation, its spokesmen recognizing the Judaic background of Christianity. Again many teachings and practices of Judaism and Christianity were incorporated into the Islamic religion. This close relationship may perhaps explain the relative ease with which men, down through history, have been converted from one of these religions to another. It may, paradoxically, also help to explain the frequent bitter quarrels among the adherents of the three religions over the question of which was the true revelation of God.

The Conquests

Moslem civilization was the product of Moslem religion. Islam transformed the important and quarreling tribes of Arabia into a dynamic world power that was to conquer one of the world's great empires within a little more than a century after the Prophet's death. When Mohammed died there was a momentary threat that the Arab community he had founded would disintegrate. Mohammed had made no provision for his own succession. Obviously no one could fill his role as the one true prophet; still the nascent Arab community needed leadership. A few Arab tribes relapsed into their old separatist tendencies and tried to withdraw from the confederation once Mohammed's personal leadership had ended. At this crucial moment some of Mohammed's companions took matters in hand and designated his father-in-law, Abu-Bakr, as "caliph," or successor to the Prophet as leader of the community. During his two-year reign (632–634) he boldly forced defecting tribes back into the community of Islam and virtually completed the political unification of the Arabs. Two other able companions, Omar (634–644) and Othman (644–656), were elected, in turn, as successors of Abu-Bakr. These succeeding caliphs led an attack on the Eastern Roman and Persian empires, neither of which proved a match for the soldiers of Allah. Riddled by internal dissension and weakened by the attacks of Heraclius, the Persian Empire was completely destroyed and its territory occupied by 650. The Eastern Roman Empire, similarly enfeebled by religious divisions and by the assaults of many enemies during the preceding half century, surrendered its eastern provinces—Syria, Palestine, and Egypt—with ridiculous ease. As a result of these victories the Arabs advanced to the shores of the Mediterranean Sea, where they soon developed a naval force and launched an attack on the very heart of the Byzantine Empire.

After Othman's death, the Arab advance was momentarily slowed because of the succession problem. The practice of electing caliphs suddenly engendered fierce conflicts among the Arabs and eventually led to civil war. Out of this strife the experienced political leader Moawiya emerged victor and in 661 founded a dynasty which came to be known as the Umayyad. Under the capable leadership of this dynasty, the internal stability of the Arab community was restored and Arab armies resumed their conquests.

The chief thrust of the Umayyads was westward across Africa. One after another the possessions of the Byzantine emperors were conquered and the Berber princes of North Africa subdued, until by the end of the seventh century Arab troops had reached the Atlantic. But they did not stop there. In 711 they crossed the Straits of Gibraltar, quickly crushed the decrepit Visigothic kingdom, and annexed all Spain except a few miniscule principalities in the mountains of the northwest. Soon Arab raiding parties began to probe across the Pyrenees into the kingdom of the Franks, but here they met a more formidable foe. In 732, exactly one hundred years after Mohammed's death, the Frankish prince, Charles Martel, defeated the Arab forces near Tours. This victory marked a significant step in the resurgence of Frankish power in Western Europe. In Arab history it signified the high tide of westward expansion. Soon after 732 the Moslems withdrew south of the Pyrenees, but not before they had established naval supremacy over the western Mediterranean, leaving Western Europe's Mediterranean shores vulnerable to their raids.

In the meantime other Arab forces pushed eastward from Persia and lopped off vast new conquests in Afghanistan, Transoxiana, Turkestan, and western India. Arab armies probed the western areas of China early in the eighth century and seemed about to absorb the ancient but decadent empire of the T'ang dynasty. The Chinese resistance, however, checked Arab advance in that direction.

During these far-flung campaigns the Umayyad princes found time and energy to hack away at the Byzantine Empire. They overran Armenia, repeatedly raided Asia Minor, and challenged Byzantine power at sea. On at least two occasions, in 674–678 and 717–718, Byzantium seemed on the brink of total destruction. But the imperial government in Constantinople, by skillful regrouping of its forces and by tapping its reserves, managed to avoid disaster. (The Moslems would not subdue Constantinople for over seven more centuries, until 1453.) The victory of the Byzantines over the Arabs in 718 was perhaps the decisive event in checking Arab expansion.

This bare enumeration of Arab conquests recounts an all but incredible achievement for a people so recently disorganized and powerless. The world had never seen so vast an empire created in a single century. By 750 no one would have disputed the emergence of a major world power capable of changing the course of history.

Internal Development

It still remains to be seen how the Arab conquerors succeeded as rulers of their huge empire. The problems of administration proved infinitely more difficult than those of conquest; but even so, the Umayyad caliphs were soon able to achieve some positive results.

During the first century after Mohammed's death his Arab followers played the predominant role in Moslem history, constituting themselves a military elite systematically levying tribute on non-Moslems, most of whom were also not Arabs, as a means of supporting the victorious sons of Allah. In general, the Arabs sought to maintain themselves apart from their subjects. Living in exclusive military cities, they tended to permit local religious practices, customs, and even governmental institutions to continue in their conquered lands. Contrary to what is often believed, they did not try to force Islam on their subjects, preferring instead to keep the true faith as their chief mark of distinction. The policy of noninterference with existing ways of life made Moslem conquest relatively painless to its victims.

For all that they conducted themselves as a military elite ruling a vast horde of subjects, the Arabs still faced the difficult task of disciplining themselves sufficiently to maintain their supremacy. Mohammed had developed a vague theocratic state in which he as Prophet exercised political authority; and his immediate successors sought to continue this tradition. Their moral authority, however, did not prove adequate to sustain such a theocracy, especially after their Arab subjects poured out over parts of three continents. The early caliphs tried to control their troops by supplementing religious ties with a pension system sanctioned by the Koran whereby each Arab warrior received a share of the booty and tribute exacted from the conquered peoples. Since this system only bred greed and disappointment, the new Umayyad dynasty, when it succeeded to power in 661, attempted to institute a more orderly system of control. Moawiya, its founder, had spent many years as governor in Syria and had observed the working of the Eastern Roman imperial system there. Once in power, he moved his capital to Damascus and proceeded to establish a bureaucratic government resembling the Roman system. The theocratic and patriarchal flavor of early Arab government gave way to a more secular state which emphasized sound organization and efficient administration. The success of this Umayyad system of government marked one of the highlights of early Moslem history, for never had the Arabs been as well organized and disciplined. By imitating the governmental techniques of more civilized peoples, the Arabs succeeded in establishing and ruling a great empire.

Conquest and political organization consumed most of the Arab energies and talents during the seventh and early eighth centuries. Aside from their religion, their language, and their poetry, the Arabs had little in the way of culture to offer to their conquered subjects, most of whom were their superiors in literature, learning, art, science, and philosophy. Down to the end of the Umayyad period in 750 their only notable cultural achievement was in the field of architecture, where they early developed a style suited to their mode of worship. Mohammed himself had built a place of worship at Medina consisting of an enclosed courtyard, partially roofed and containing a pulpit from which he could preach and lead services of prayer. This prototype provided a ground plan for the mosque which was imitated in one conquered city after another. The mosques built in the Umayyad period, however, became increasingly elaborate under the influence of local styles of architecture. The Arab masters employed native artisans who applied techniques and ideas derived from their experiences in building places of worship for their previous Christian, Jewish, and Zoroastrian masters. In this way several notable mosques were built by Umayyad princes, perhaps the most famous being the mosque in Jerusalem, called the Dome of the Rock, or sometimes in error the Mosque of Omar. Built by an Umayyad caliph determined to create a Moslem structure more splendid than the Christian Church of the Holy Sepulcher, the Dome of the Rock embodied many features of Byzantine architectural style, especially its dome and its brilliantly colored mosaics. At Damascus, another splendid mosque was characterized by local influences, in this case its distinctive minarets. Persian, Indian, and Greek artisans all shared in its building. But aside from the effort of the Arabs to create places of worship suitable to their religious practices, they brought few cultural contributions to their conquered territories during the Umayyad period. Most of the old cultural life of the non-Arab population of the Moslem Empire persisted unchanged. The masters borrowed things here and there as suited their needs, but pressing military and political problems left them little time or energy for cultural affairs.

And yet this was a period of incubation preparatory to the brilliant cultural renaissance that broke over the Moslem world in the eighth century. Of prime importance in this development was the spread of the Moslem religion from Spain to India. Not only did the Arabs themselves range over this huge area as representatives of Islam, but large numbers of non-Arabs began to accept the religion of the conquerors. By 750, Egypt and Persia were predominately Moslem, while in Syria there were numerous converts mixed with the Christians and the Jews. Even in the more distant provinces the number of converts mounted steadily. The conversions were not primarily the result of any compulsion or even missionary activity by the conquerors, who seemed content to retain their religion as an Arab monopoly. Nor was there any great advantage to be gained by conversion. During the Umayyad period the ruling Arabs generally taxed non-Arabs and excluded them from political and military life even if they did accept Islam. Most of the converts would seem to have been won over by the religious teachings of Mohammed, aided by the similarity between Islam and the other existing religions which made conversion relatively easy.

The spread of Islam inevitably stimulated cultural exchange and growth. As the Arab Moslems encountered other cultures, they found it increasingly necessary to weigh them against their religious ideas; and as non-Arabs accepted Islam they were faced with the problem of readjusting their old cultural values to the teachings of the new religion. The resulting synthesis provided the impetus for the creation of a vast new Moslem culture. The spread of Arabic as a common language provided the instrumentality for its development and diffusion. Although the Arabs did not impose their language on their subjects, it was widely adopted during the Umayyad period, since Moslem custom discouraged the translation of the Koran, thereby forcing all who wished to adhere to the new faith to learn Arabic.

Thus during the first century of Moslem history the Arabs put themselves in position to become heirs to all the earlier civilizations existing in the lands they had conquered. As Moslems, however, they were obliged to judge whether the foreign cultures met God's approval, which meant that they had to scrutinize all aspects of cultural life within their empire. Synthesis was clearly the logical outcome of this situation; and, though this monumental task was not completed immediately, nevertheless Arab conquest and the spread of the Moslem religion prior to 750 had set the stage.

Beyond question, during the first century of its history Islam had rudely shaken the Mediterranean world. A new religion and a new military power had erupted to revolutionize the religious and political geography of large areas in Africa, Asia, and Europe. The emergence of this new power placed older states and religions in extreme jeopardy. And the internal conditions within the new empire presaged a vast cultural upheaval and a new alignment of spiritual forces. The birth of Islam in the seventh century pointed toward a new chapter in history.

Western European Society

Certainly the main interest in the seventh and early eighth centuries is concentrated in the eastern Mediterranean area, where the remnant of the old Roman Empire assured its continued existence by a radical regrouping of its political, social, and moral resources, and where a militant new power emerged and grew strong by utilizing the resources of older civilizations. Over Western Europe there hung an air of stagnation and retrogression on all levels of life, suggesting that the barbarian mode of existence had finally gained the upper hand. The gloom of this situation seemed to deepen as the period wore on, and yet even in the midst of so many difficulties one can discern signs that Western European society was slowly finding solid foundations upon which to construct its own peculiar way of life.

Political Chaos

Probably the most dismal aspect of Western European life after 600 was the decay of governmental institutions and the consequent reign of violence. By the end of the sixth century four Germanic groups dominated Western Europe: the Anglo-Saxons in Britain, the Franks in Gaul, the Visigoths in Spain, and the Lombards in Italy. The political history of Western Europe in the early Middle Ages presents a grim record of war, court intrigue, and grave injustice. And this general state of disorder was too often attributable to the conduct of the rulers of the Germanic kingdoms. Out of the depressing story of political affairs, however, certain broad conclusions about the nature of Western European political life in this dark age do emerge.

The Germanic rulers contended with immense problems which militated against the establishment of sound political order. As a minority which had established a dominant position by conquest, they could command little moral authority over their subjects. Since the boundaries of their states were usually ill-defined, they were involved in endemic warfare to gain new or defend old territory, especially in England, where several small Germanic kingdoms coexisted in a state of perpetual warfare, and in Italy, where after 568 the Lombards competed incessantly with the Byzantine emperors for control of the peninsula. In addition, they were subject to repeated attacks by foreign invaders. The Arabs began the destruction of the Visigothic kingdom in 711, and Slavic hordes continually harassed the Franks along their eastern frontier. Finally, the Germanic rulers faced the unhappy task of governing a population that had once enjoyed and still remembered the services supplied by the highly organized, essentially humane imperial regime of Rome; any comparison between the old Roman Empire and the new barbarian kingdoms could not but discredit the Germans.

In spite of the magnitude of the task most Germanic rulers tried, during the sixth century, to organize their kingdoms on the model of the Roman government that had preceded them. So great were their efforts, if not their lasting achievements, that one authority on early mediaeval institutions has argued that the Germanic invasions caused no real change in Roman civilization. Exaggerated as this claim unquestionably is, some of the early Germanic regimes seemed to promise a stable political order not radically different from that maintained by Rome.

The Germanic princes, however, were too little removed from barbarism to make such a transition; and these early promises were not fulfilled during the seventh and early eighth centuries. The ambitious monarchical regimes of the sixth century were little more than facades hiding a wide variety of grave political ills. The kingdom of the Franks in Gaul under the Merovingian dynasty might well serve to illustrate the fate of Germanic states founded within the territory of the moribund empire.

Merovingian history impresses the reader with nothing so much as the contrast between the pretensions and the powers of its kings. All successors of Clovis (481–511), the founder of the dynasty, claimed absolute authority, but between the end of the sixth and the middle of the eighth centuries their actual power dwindled away to nothing. The causes of this decline were numerous. Most of the Merovingians, incapable of surmounting their barbarian political tradition, created an atmosphere of violence and tyranny by their unmitigated use of force to gain their political ends. Few royal dynasties in all history can match the record of violence and brutality of the rulers of the last half of the sixth century, as recorded by the contemporary bishop of Tours, Gregory, in his *History of the Franks*. Even more ferocious were their wives, especially Brunhilda, a Visigothic princess married to King Sigebert and referred to by her contemporaries as "the second Jezebel," and Fredegunde, the slave mistress of King Chilperic, who became his queen after strangling his first wife, the sister of Brunhilda. Fredegunde subsequently fanned the hatred of Brunhilda even more by arranging the murder of

Sigebert and by urging Chilperic to seize the inheritance of Brunhilda's sons. The numerous acts of violence of these indomitable queens, perpetrated to further the interests of their husbands and offspring, dominate the history of the last part of the sixth and the early years of the seventh centuries. Perhaps the only excuse for their conduct was the fact that scheming relatives and greedy nobles goaded them to crime by equally heinous deeds. At least these figures were dynamic and forceful, which is more than can be said for the succession of kings who ascended to the throne in the last half of the seventh and early eighth centuries. Debauched by the excesses of the court at an early age, they usually died while still in their thirties, and were followed by sons of the same despicable character.

Having only the vaguest notion of public welfare, the kings seldom attempted anything resembling positive services for their subjects. In accordance with ancient Germanic custom they treated the state as private property to be divided among all their male heirs, thus breeding vicious family quarrels that consumed their energies and frequently flared into devastating civil wars. By the end of the seventh century, repeated partition had fragmented the once unified Merovingian state into at least four separate kingdoms. And even on those rare occasions when a Merovingian ruler sought to rise above greedy ambition and petty quarrels and develop some constructive program, he found himself frustrated by the bewildering array of laws, customs, religious practices, languages, and levels of culture which rendered impossible the application of any single policy to all his subjects.

Thus the Merovingians—plagued by barbarian habits, lack of resources, inadequate concepts of government, and a multiplicity of other problems—never succeeded in dominating their situation. In the derisive words of a ninth-century author they became "do-nothing" kings, content to ride in open carts from one of their private estates to another, and to intrigue among their kinsmen for bits of territory. Incapable of establishing peace and order, by their very failure they fostered the spread of that anarchy within which the new political institutions of Western Europe were to take root.

Unable to provide more than a rudimentary government themselves, the Merovingian kings were forced to share political power with the great landowners. The rise of the landed nobles to political power was a tortuous process; it was also a development of such fundamental importance that it distinguished Western Europe sharply from either Byzantium or Islam. Beginning during the last days of the Roman Empire, this development was accelerated under the Germanic kings, chiefly because they lacked sufficient money income to support the services of government. Their only recourse was to call upon their subjects to render political services at private expense, especially in military expeditions, in the maintenance of internal peace and order, and in the administration of justice. Only the wealthy could respond, and they demanded as a price for their services additional grants of lands from the private estates of the king and the right to govern their own estates as private realms. By this process the kings depleted their resources and divided their power; at the same time the nobles acquired more land, instituted private governments, and subjected the bulk of the population to their immediate authority. The kings tried to ensure the loyalty of the landowners by requiring of each a personal oath of allegiance, a process called commendation, which placed the nobles in a special category above the mass of the people and forced the kings to devote their major energies to guarding their position against the encroachments of their powerful vassals.

These early steps in the evolution of what eventually was to be called the feudal system caused tremendous strife. The line between the authority of the king and the nobles was so indefinite as to ensure a continual struggle between them. The new system nevertheless provided a basis for the restoration of order. The powerful nobles, each entrenched in a small area, could protect and control the population in their immediate localities. Yet above them stood the king as a source of their authority and a symbol of the commonalty of the larger group. This system was primitive compared to the contemporary regimes of the Byzantine emperors or the Umayyad caliphs, but under it the West began to develop its own characteristic political organization.

Economic and Social Development

Western Europe also suffered a gradual but desperate economic depression between 600 and 750. Its causes have been much disputed, being attributed in turn to the economic backwardness of the Germans, the cutting of the Mediterranean trade routes by the Arabs, the financial abuses of the late Roman emperors, and the failure of manpower. If the causes are confused, the manifestations of depression were clear. Trade fell off steadily until by mid-eighth century, it was practically nonexistent. The failure of trade paralyzed city life. It was not uncommon for seventh-century observers to complain that grass was growing in the streets of the blighted cities. Traders and artisans disappeared and with them went a considerable part of the technical competence of the West.

The population of once-thriving cities was forced to resort to agriculture as a means of livelihood; land became virtually the only source of wealth, and the old money economy vanished. Agricultural life centered increasingly around the large, often huge, estates known as latifundia or manors which were already nearly self-sufficient. The heirs of the old aristocratic landowners who had once played an important part in the economic and cultural life of the cities now tended to spend most of their lives on their estates. Small farmers deprived of markets, not to mention police protection, together with wandering refugees from the dying cities now made up the labor force on the landlords' estates, in return for which they received small parcels of land to be used for their own livelihood. Numerous forces combined to create a social order in which members of this peasantry were required by law or custom to remain attached to the estates on which they were born, thereby producing the new status of serfdom.

The decline of trade and urban life and the growing dependence on an agriculture which was centered in isolated estates drastically reduced the standard of living of Western European society, hastened its division into two classes of landlord and serf, and fostered an extreme provincialism of outlook. In these ways Western Europe contrasted sharply with the more prosperous and diversified societies of the Byzantine and Moslem worlds, and its economic and social backwardness was destined to last for several centuries.

Religious Life in Western Europe

While the Germanic kingdoms of Western Europe painfully constructed a new basis for their society in a political order which was dominated by landed aristocracy and an economic system which was comprised of self-sufficient manors, their religious institutions were undergoing a comparable transformation—a transformation that was to produce a Christian establishment fitted to the needs of the time and confined to the geographical area of the West.

Perhaps it is fitting to recall here that prior to 600 A.D. the church had already developed its basic organization, doctrine, liturgy, and moral code. These aspects of Christian life had survived the decay of the Roman world amazingly well, thus giving the church tremendous resources with which to face the new age. As was suggested in the discussion of Christian life in the eastern Mediterranean, the most significant religious development during the seventh and eighth centuries was the division of Christendom into separate "churches" and the consequent modification of established institutions to fit them into their new compartments.

The church in Western Europe was set apart from other churches by virtue of the fact that from the fifth century onward it could no longer rely on the beneficent support of a strong government. The Germanic princes were Christian and tended to support the church, but they usually harmed and weakened it by their brutal methods and political ineptness. Instinctively they fostered the growth of "national" churches within their realms, thereby further disrupting such unity of Western Christendom as might have survived the decentralization and disintegration of society. At the same time the religious leadership of the bishops was severely strained by the growing wealth of the church. Since the bulk of that wealth was necessarily in land, the bishops became landlords and inevitably assumed the political duties that were becoming inseparable from the control of large estates. Their political and economic duties absorbed most of their energies, leaving little time for their religious responsibilities. Because the office carried wealth and power, competition for episcopal sees became vicious, the strong usually winning over the pious. The typical bishop of the seventh and eighth centuries was a warlike, worldly figure not overly concerned with spiritual affairs, and his shortcomings were reflected in the declining quality of his priests. These men were unlettered, ignorant of the rudiments of doctrine, unfamiliar with liturgy, and lax in moral life, and since it was they who represented the church in the parishes it was not surprising that superstitions, pagan usages, and gross immorality characterized the lives of the great mass of the people. Christianity no less than the other aspects of Western civilization was barbarized by the Germanic invasions.

At just the moment when barbarism permeated religious life most seriously, new divisions weakened the unity of Christendom. Issues of dogma and discipline were beginning to pull the Byzantine church away from the Western tradition. Although the schism was still not complete by 750, mutual exchange was increasingly tenuous, and the possibility of *rapprochement* was seriously reduced by the inability of the Byzantine state to protect its Italian holdings and maintain free communication between the West and Byzantium. The Moslem seizure of Armenia, Syria, Palestine, Egypt, North Africa, and Spain, which was accompanied by extensive conversion of Christians to Islam, represented not merely a serious reduction of the Christian population but, in addition, a cruel blow to Christian unity. It limited the relationships between the numerous Christians of these areas and those of Western Europe to a rare and generally unfruitful exchange of letters between bishops or an occasional Western pilgrimage to Jerusalem. Western

Christians were, in effect, cut off from the rest of the Christian world.

Confronted with difficult problems caused by the barbarization of society, and isolated increasingly from other Christian communities, the church in the West faced a serious crisis. It did, however, succeed in finding ways of dealing with some of its problems which were to contribute in an extremely important way to the development of the mediaeval church.

In an age of weak and aimless rulers, secular governments abandoned all responsibility for the welfare of their subjects. The church, with more positive leadership, shouldered the burden of caring for the weak. It maintained the only existing hospitals and schools. Its ideas of justice and mercy penetrated and tempered the harsh Germanic law codes. Educated clergymen served kings in numerous political capacities, thereby putting the church's stamp on political development. As its participation in social activity broadened, the prestige of the church increased. As a consequence it played an incalculably important role in shaping new standards of social welfare and reawakening the social consciousness of Western Europe.

Another accomplishment of the church was its continued success in winning converts through the efforts of its missionaries. The process of converting the Germanic nations who had invaded the Roman Empire was finally completed during the seventh century with the Anglo-Saxons in England. Although both Irish and Roman missionaries exerted strong influences in England, the Roman forces eventually predominated, especially in organizing the new converts and in instituting the outward practices of the church. Throughout the seventh century, Irish missionaries labored to destroy pockets of paganism on the continent, especially along the eastern frontier of the Frankish kingdom. Early in the eighth century English missionaries directed by the papacy penetrated the trans-Rhine area and began the conversion of Germanic groups that had never invaded the old Roman Empire. The missionaries operating in these areas represented the force of civilization assaulting barbarism on barbarian soil and made Christianity a basis for communication between the German leaders within the old empire and those without. Through these efforts the nascent Western European civilization began to spread and to develop. Under proper leadership, religious reform could be more easily instituted where the church was newly established than where it was already bound by tradition. England, for example, became the center of piety and learning for the whole West during the seventh and early eighth centuries, and her churchmen exercised a strong influence outside of England as well. In a somewhat similar way missionary work also offered the bishop of Rome an opportunity to organize new territory under his jurisdiction, and thereby increase his authority.

Overshadowing, however, both the extension of its role in society and the expansion of its jurisdiction into new geographical areas was the achievement of the church in producing institutions capable of restoring discipline within Christian society and of deepening its spiritual life. In this respect the seventh and early eighth centuries were especially important because of the growth of the papacy and the spread of the Benedictine monastic order.

The papacy had established itself as an important force in Christendom long before the seventh century. Guarding the tradition that Rome was the prime episcopacy in Christendom by virtue of Christ's commission to Peter and Peter's subsequent choice of Rome as his see, the bishops of Rome had slowly built up a reputation as a source of doctrinal orthodoxy and proper disciplinary regulation. They had acquired extensive wealth and played an important role in political life in Italy, especially during the era of the Germanic invasions and the collapse of Roman government. During the sixth century, however, the power and prestige of the papacy was threatened first by the resurgent power of the Eastern Roman Empire and then by the invading Lombards. Justinian's conquest of Italy placed a political master over the popes, a master who insisted on dictating religious policy and who responded to Roman claims to supremacy by supporting the counterclaims of the patriarch of Constantinople. Then in 568 the Lombard invasion thrust the Italian peninsula into war and constantly threatened the capture of Rome. Papal influence was also weakened by the strong tendency of Germanic kings to assert control of the churches within their lands.

At this critical juncture the Roman papacy was saved from these menacing forces by the inspiring genius of Pope Gregory the Great (590–604). Descended from a noble family, the young Gregory received a good education designed to prepare him for service in the imperial government. He soon abandoned his public career, however, to become a monk, which by his own admission was all that he ever desired to be. He was drawn into the service of the papacy as a legate to Constantinople and then elevated to the papal office in 590, chiefly because of the demands of the Roman populace, agitated at the moment by a terrible plague. Throughout his pontificate he remained the good shepherd to his Roman flock, gathering grain to feed them, lifting up their spirits with powerful sermons, and organizing various activities to relieve the miseries of the sick and the helpless. His talents found more than a local application, however.

A man of deep religious fervor and hardheaded practical sense, Gregory launched a policy of making the papacy politically and economically independent while increasing its spiritual leadership in the Christian world. To lay the basis for political and economic independence he husbanded the papal property in Italy. To reduce papal dependence on any outside political power, he maneuvered to become a mediating force in the Italian struggles between the Lombard kings and the Byzantine emperors. But his efforts to create an independent secular power did not exhaust his energies. Gregory earned his greatest fame as a spiritual leader, especially gifted in stating Christian doctrine in a language suitable to the mentality of Western Europe. His sermons, his commentaries on Scripture, his pastoral instructions, and his inspirational writings became a basic part of the religious tradition in the West and everywhere served to deepen spiritual life. He showed an interest in refining Christian liturgy and establishing a standard usage. He was responsible for directing a missionary party to England which succeeded not only in winning numerous converts but also in organizing them under Roman leadership. Under his guidance the Roman see assumed a new prominence throughout all Christendom. And yet it is clear that Gregory's policy of building papal authority was a step in the direction of creating a separate Western church. His attempts to escape any dependence on the Byzantine Empire, his simple writings in Latin, his careful efforts to tie newly converted peoples to Rome all tended to confine and concentrate the effective leadership of the papacy to the West.

Although none of Gregory's successors approached his achievements, all continued his policy and contributed to the development of the papacy. During the eighth century they enjoyed notable missionary successes among the Germans east of the Rhine. They also took an active interest in spiritual and moral reform, particularly within the Frankish church. In addition, their efforts in the definition of dogma and the promulgation of a uniform ritual were so successful that it is usual to speak of "Roman" Christianity spreading in the seventh and eighth centuries. This aspect of papal activity was notably demonstrated in its triumphant resistance to the iconoclastic decrees of the Byzantine emperors. In this context continued adherence to Gregory's idea of papal independence was particularly important. Although still nominally subject to Byzantium, the popes were able to escape close control by playing the Lombards off against the emperors. When, however, the emperors became increasingly concerned with problems in the east, the popes found themselves at the mercy of the Lombards and only escaped their domination by persuading the Franks to assume a protectorate over the papacy. An event of incalculable significance, this alliance inextricably bound the popes to a western policy and reinforced the position of the papacy in Western Europe.

The evolving role of the papacy as an independent political force and spiritual leader in the west was also greatly assisted by the spread of Benedictine monasticism. Christian asceticism, stressing withdrawal from worldly affairs in order to serve God better, had originated in the east as early as the third century and had flowered in many forms in succeeding years. In the west this manifestation of Christian piety was channeled into a unique and admirable form by the genius of St. Benedict of Nursia (480–543). Born an

Italian nobleman, he gave up a promising public career to become a monk. Eventually he founded a monastery at Monte Cassino in Italy, where he devised his famous Benedictine rule to guide the daily life of the members of his community. The essence of this rule was contained in the idea that God could best be served by a community of dedicated men who divided their energies between prayer, study, and manual labor. To maintain the necessary discipline the rule gave the abbot extensive authority over the community. It also required the monks to take vows of poverty, chastity, and obedience, thereby cutting them off from the material, personal, and political problems of the outside world and freeing them to concentrate their energies on the work of the monastery and the worship of God.

Benedict's rule was adopted by monastic communities throughout most of Western Europe during the sixth, seventh, and eighth centuries, thus creating an elite corps of "soldiers of Christ" whose services to the barbarized society in which they operated were incalculable. Of these services perhaps the most important was the example the Benedictine monks set for piety and moral excellence. They were especially fitted for the role of leadership in religious reform. They helped to guide the bewildered Europeans in the proper performance of the Roman ritual and played a major role in its dissemination. They served as teachers, transmitting to the ignorant a deeper understanding of the basic tenets of the Christian faith, and they led in the reorganization of charitable activities. Along with the Gospel, they also spread among their pagan neighbors technical knowledge and skill, their well organized monastic estates serving as models of good farming. All of these developments followed from the peculiar nature of the Benedictine rule, with its emphasis on a communal life of moderation, balance, and discipline. Perhaps the ascetics in the east excelled the Benedictines in an ability to perform feats of physical self-denial (for instance, sitting atop a pillar for thirty years, as did St. Simeon Stylites) or in a grasp of the intricacies of advanced theology; but the Benedictine glory lay in their singular ability to grapple with the peculiar religious problems of the West.

On the whole, then, this was an era of considerable creative activity in western Christendom starting with the emergence of a Western European church able to exist in its own right. No one, of course, had abandoned belief in the existence of a universal community of Christians, but the divisive forces of the period seemed clearly to be fragmenting universal Christendom and favoring the development of separate churches, each with its own institutions and orientation.

Cultural Development

Amidst the difficulties besetting Western Europe after 600 A.D. one would not be surprised by a decay of arts and letters. The seventh and early eighth centuries were in general characterized by a decline in the level of cultural life in Western Europe. The remnants of Latin culture were badly neglected, and there was little of freshness or vigor to take its place. The weight of barbarism, political chaos, violence, isolation, and poverty bore too heavily on society to permit any great creative activity, and the period has thus become known as a "Dark Age."

Yet this generalization must be qualified, for there were some positive developments, among them the efforts to preserve parts of classical culture. Benedictine monks, taking seriously their founder's order to study, laboriously copied the works of classical authors and the church fathers for their tiny libraries. To use these works they needed Latin, and therefore compiled simple textbooks for its study. Schools were established to teach the rudimentary knowledge needed to carry on monastic study. A tenuous link was thus maintained with the dying classical world, a fact of major importance to later Western Europe. Under certain favorable conditions, especially in newly established Benedictine monasteries, a few individuals were able to study and write. In the early seventh century Spain produced an outstanding man of learning in Isidore, bishop of Seville. Beside writing important theological tracts, Isidore compiled a huge encyclopedia, called *Etymologies*, consisting of scraps of knowledge drawn from a wide range of classical authors and pertaining to numerous different subjects. For several centuries it was a popular source of information among scholars throughout the West. A brilliant cultural life was also sustained in Irish monasteries in this period. Irish scholars even retained an ability to use Greek long after it had disappeared elsewhere in the West. Irish manuscript illuminations of this era represent the finest art work of the early Middle Ages. Some of the Irish enthusiasm for learning was transported to England by missionaries. In late seventh-century and early eighth-century England there emerged a long line of monastic scholars who produced histories, theological discussions, poetry, Biblical commentaries, and even scientific tracts. Bede was the most famous of these English scholars, his influence being felt all over the West. His *Ecclesiastical History of the English People*, which traces the institution of Christianity in England, supplies a remarkably full picture of the condition of life in the semibarbarian Western world of the sixth, seventh, and early eighth centuries; moreover, it sets an exceptionally high standard of accuracy and good literary style. These islands of intellectual and literary activity prevented total sterility in Western European cultural life and served as a base upon which future cultural achievements would be constructed.

The dominance of the church in Western Europe's feeble intellectual life was in itself a vital development, for the clerical and monastic scholars inevitably selected the aspects of classical culture that suited their religious and moral convictions while disregarding what was more secular. They tended to devote their creative energies to pursuits that were religious while neglecting other channels of thought, art, and literary expression. Over the course of time this selective activity definitely "Christianized" and "clericized" culture and supplied the church with a virtual monopoly of the content and orientation of cultural development which became a distinguishing feature of Western European civilization for many centuries.

Between 600 and 750 the world about which Gregory the Great was so apprehensive had found a new orientation. The Roman heritage had been divided into three portions: Byzantine, Moslem, and Western European, each containing vital new forces that could not be contained within the old framework, itself badly weakened by internal ills. The new forces were so effervescent that by 750 the fate of historical development was by no means decided, although a direction had been established. The vast changes, however, had not eradicated the old Graeco-Roman tradition, for imbedded in each of the new civilizations was a residue of classical institutions and outlooks destined to supply vital nourishment to their future development.

CHAPTER II

The Revival of the West

TOWARD the middle of the eighth century a certain degree of political stability seemed to be re-emerging in the lands encircling the Mediterranean Sea. The most active forces during the preceding era of rapid transformation had been the Germans, Slavs, Avars, Bulgars, and Arabs, all of whom rained sledge-hammer blows on the civilized world. By 750 their invasions seemed to have been curbed and the danger of the complete destruction of civilization averted. The Byzantines had been especially effective in containing these attacks; by conserving and organizing their strength, they had saved their empire and by mid-eighth century stood like a bulwark against further barbarian invasion. At the same time the invaders ceased to threaten. The most potent of all, the Arabs, showed signs of running out of offensive power and of being willing to settle for what they had already won. The various Germanic states in Western Europe appeared even less menacing; politically disorganized, economically impoverished, culturally barbarous, and morally backward, they certainly seemed incapable of disturbing the equilibrium of the Mediterranean area.

The promised stability, however, did not materialize. Instead, about 750 the new balance of the Mediterranean world was suddenly shattered by the explosive emergence of a dynamic power in Western Europe. Behind the transformation of the Frankish kingdom into a major power by the Carolingian dynasty were social, religious, and cultural developments which served notice that the increased influence of the West was more than a flourish of naked power by Germanic war lords. Especially significant in the strengthening of the West was the role of the church. Under Carolingian leadership Western Europe finally became cognizant of its peculiarities and strove harder than ever to give expression to them in its own institutions.

The decline of militant expansionism among the Moslems after 750 provided a welcome relief to the Arabs' old foes, especially the "second Rome" on the Bosporus. Moslem society underwent radical internal changes, leading toward the creation of a cosmopolitan civilization to replace the nationalistic Arab society of the heroic age of conquest. The brilliance of this new Moslem civilization, however, cast a shadow over Byzantium's role as world cultural leader. And under Carolingian leadership, Western Europe repeatedly challenged or ignored Byzantium's already badly shaken claims of political, religious, and cultural authority over Christendom. Thus, whereas the era from 600 to 750 was characterized chiefly by a physical shrinkage of the Byzantine world, the era extending from 750 to 850 witnessed a corresponding diminution of Byzantine prestige.

Rise and Greatness of the Carolingians as a World Power, 714–840

Shortly after his death in 814, Charlemagne's achievement was commemorated by the following epitaph: "Beneath this tomb rests the body of Charles, the great and orthodox emperor who nobly extended the kingdom of the

Franks and ruled prosperously for forty-seven years. . . ."
Whoever formulated this tribute came close to summarizing the essential features of the whole range of early Carolingian achievements. For the history of Western Europe
between the early eighth century and about 840 is primarily
a story of how a new family became "great" in the eyes of
the world through conquests, good and prosperous government, and vigorous support of the true faith.

Origins of the Carolingian Family

It has been previously noted that the Merovingian dynasty of the Frankish kingdom declined during the seventh
and early eighth centuries until its scions were fittingly
called "do-nothing" kings. Before they were formally replaced, their authority had been usurped by the rising
Carolingian family. Having gained prominence in the seventh century by acquiring extensive estates in Austrasia,
the Carolingians soon achieved greater prestige than any
other noble family by establishing hereditary control of the
position of mayor of the palace in the service of the Merovingian rulers of that subkingdom in the northeastern part
of the Frankish realm. The chief responsibility of this office
was the management and disposition of the royal lands; and
through its systematic exploitation over a considerable period the Carolingians managed to build up a strong following. By extending to the Austrasian nobles parcels of royal
lands in return for loyal support, the Carolingian mayors of
the palace succeeded in commanding greater loyalty among
the nobles than did the weak kings.

The ambitious mayors next launched their forces beyond
Austrasia into the conflicts raging among the various
branches of the Merovingian family. Success in this venture came to Pepin of Heristal, the first Carolingian who

stands out clearly in history. Posing as a champion of the Merovingian king of Austrasia whom he served as mayor of the palace, Pepin waged war on the mayor of the palace of Neustria, who was trying to exalt his branch of the Merovingian royal family. In 687 by virtue of a decisive military victory, Pepin established dominance over Neustria and then over Burgundy. His victory not only checked the territorial disintegration of the Frankish state and reinstituted a single political regime, but enabled him to serve as mayor of the palace for the reunited Merovingian kingdom.

The Carolingians gained new prominence under Charles Martel, son of Pepin and mayor of the palace from 714 to 741. Charles's policy is very well summed up by the sobriquet "Martel," which means "the Hammer." For Charles was essentially a ruthless warrior who crushed internal resistance to the authority of the monarch and beat back foreign attackers. His chief victims within the boundaries of the Frankish kingdom were great noble families who sought to defy the authority of the crown. Although the Carolingians themselves had only recently risen to power by usurping their kings' authority and wealth, under Charles Martel the family switched its policy to a jealous protection of royal power against the ambitions of the nobility. In order to subdue nobles and to defend the frontiers Charles Martel concentrated military power in his own hands as mayor of the palace. The problem of defense was complicated by a change in methods of warfare which saw the infantryman replaced by the armored cavalryman as the main element of an army. Charles solved the two basic problems inherent in this military transformation by building up a body of loyal vassals bound to the king and his mayor of the palace by oaths of personal loyalty and large grants of land, some of it taken from the church.

The land was not merely intended to attach the nobles to the king but to make it possible for them to support the crushing expense—under prevailing economic conditions— of feeding their chargers and of devoting themselves almost exclusively to training in the difficult art of fighting in the saddle. Finally the land was retained by the nobles only so long as they were loyal in the performance of the expensive services they owed. So successful was Charles in developing this revolutionary fighting force that he was able to win impressive victories over formidable foreign opponents. His most famous victory came in 732 near Tours, when he defeated a Moslem raiding party, but nearly as impressive were his victories over the pagan Saxons and Frisians, who menaced the northeastern frontier of the kingdom. By the end of his life Charles was widely respected. Although he was still only mayor of the palace, he used his personal power to run the kingdom as he saw fit. The Carolingians were in fact masters of a large state although as yet they wore no crown.

Pepin the Short (741–768)

The prestige of the Carolingians continued to grow under Charles Martel's successor, Pepin the Short. Never for a moment abandoning Martel's policy of ruthless suppression of those who resisted central authority and of stout defense of the frontiers, Pepin succeeded in broadening Carolingian policy in several significant directions.

Probably most important was his active support of the most progressive religious forces of the era. Frankish rulers had traditionally posed as protectors of Christianity. However, Merovingian efforts in that direction had not had the happiest results; the kings' policy encouraged the growth of a Frankish national church which had little connection with the rest of the Christian world and extended the practice of secularizing church offices and property. The outcome was a deepening corruption of religious life which reached scandalous proportions early in the eighth century. Almost from the moment they gained power the Carolingians manifested an inclination to assist the church in resolving its problems. Pepin of Heristal, Charles Martel, and Carloman (Pepin the Short's brother, who shared the office of mayor of the palace with Pepin briefly) all gave active support to missionary effort. Charles Martel and Carloman also aided Boniface, an English Benedictine, in his missionary efforts to organize bishoprics, recruit priests, and found monasteries among the newly Christianized lands along the eastern frontier of the Frankish kingdom. Pepin continued this tradition by helping to initiate religious reform. Guided largely by Boniface, who was acting under papal orders, Pepin attempted to strengthen church organization, improve the quality of the clergy, end pagan practices, and deepen Christian piety. As a consequence, the papacy began to enjoy a larger role in the affairs of the Frankish kingdom. Although the task of reforming the Frankish church was much too overwhelming to complete for decades, Pepin and his family began immediately to garner prestige as servants of religion, thus adding an important new honor to their already great reputation as warriors and administrators.

Pepin's religious policy went even farther than accepting responsibility for the welfare of the Frankish church; before the end of his reign he had shouldered the burden of protecting the papacy, a responsibility that implied a pro-

tectorate over all Western Christendom. The alliance between Rome and the Franks arose out of their mutual need
for assistance. Probably the popes' need was the greater.
Since the time of Gregory the Great (590–604) the papacy
aspired to some degree of temporal independence in Italy
as a buttress for its spiritual pre-eminence; and what political strength it was able to muster was based in large part
on its territorial possessions in Italy. The popes, however,
not being strong enough to retain those possessions by
themselves, were forced to rely on the protection of an outside power. For about a century after Gregory's pontificate
the Byzantine emperors acted as papal protectors. They allowed the papacy considerable latitude in managing its affairs in Rome and the immediate environs and at the same
time held back the aggressive Lombards, who constantly
threatened the Italian territories of both emperors and
popes. Occasionally the popes sought to improve their position by playing the Lombards off against the Byzantines,
but in general they relied on Constantinople for protection.
Early in the eighth century this arrangement began to
break down. The Byzantine emperors, staggering under
the blows of the Moslems, found it more and more difficult
to fulfill their traditional role in Italy and were forced to
leave the papacy increasingly to the mercy of the Lombards. Finally after 726, when the papacy condemned the
iconoclastic policy of the emperors, co-operation between
the papacy and the emperors became virtually impossible.
The Lombards were not slow to take advantage of Byzantine weakness and the religious quarrel between Rome and
Constantinople to seize papal possessions in Italy.

Faced with the Lombard threat and the unreliability of
their traditional protectors, the popes inevitably turned to
the rising Carolingian mayors of the palace, who had al-

ready shown themselves favorably inclined toward the papacy in missionary and reforming work. To the initial papal appeals for military aid, Charles Martel made no reply. Pepin, however, was of a different mind. Perhaps he found it difficult to resist the popes, who by the 740's were proclaiming to the whole world that Pepin alone could save the territory and the independence of the see of St. Peter.

Pepin also had problems of his own which required the collaboration of the bishop of Rome. Still only mayor of the palace, he served kings who did nothing while he fought the wars, kept the peace, and promoted the true religion. To change this preposterous situation, however, involved a serious risk of rebellion. The Franks, like all Germans, believed that God had bestowed a special sanctity on those who carried royal blood in their veins and that to bestow the crown on any but a member of the royal family was sacrilege. The Carolingians were not of royal blood and therefore it was unthinkable in the customary scheme of things to depose even a do-nothing Merovingian and elect an upstart such as Pepin to the kingship. Brute strength to carry out the change of dynasty was not enough, and Pepin therefore sought some authority whose approval of his act would supply the necessary aura of legality and receive wide acceptance. The bishop of Rome seemed to meet these exacting specifications. In 749 Pepin sent a legate to Rome requesting a papal opinion about a change of dynasty, and the pope answered that "it is better that the man who has the real power should have the title of king instead of the man who has the mere title but no power." With this sanction, the Frankish nobles elected Pepin king of the Franks in 751; and the papal legate, Boniface, anointed the new king. This ceremony, never previously employed by the Franks, was probably based on the Old Testament passage describing the anointment of Saul by Samuel and signified to contemporaries that Pepin was more than king in the old tribal sense. He was king by the grace of God. The prestige of the Carolingians had been elevated to new heights; they had become kings of the Franks instead of mayors of the palace and had received a special designation from the greatest ecclesiastical authority in Christendom. With one stroke they had become unique among rulers in the West.

The alliance between popes and Carolingians was drawn still tighter in the years immediately following Pepin's elevation. Lombard pressure on the papal states increased steadily, finally culminating in 751 in the seizure of Byzantine holdings in northern Italy and a direct attack on Rome. In desperation Pope Stephen II (752–757) undertook the hazardous trip across the Alps in midwinter. Reaching Gaul early in 754, he was received with great respect by Pepin and after a series of discussions was given assurance of aid. In a solemn church ceremony Stephen personally consecrated the Frankish king, his queen, and his sons, obviously attempting to increase the prestige of the recently crowned family. Pepin in return made a promise to restore certain territories in Italy claimed by the papacy, but exactly what territories is not now clear. Apparently Stephen had confronted Pepin with the famous Donation of Constantine. This document, probably forged for the occasion, was compiled from legends current in the eighth century. Purporting to be an edict issued by Constantine at the time that he moved his capital to Constantinople in 330, it stated that the emperor turned over to the pope full authority to rule the West, together with specific possession of Rome and Italy. Since Pepin apparently had promised to restore these territories in some degree, the pope completed the new arrangement by granting him the title of "Patrician of the Romans." Previously the Latin title "patricius" had designated a Byzantine official holding certain powers, in Rome and other imperial cities, which could only be granted by the emperor. Stephen, of course, had no idea of making Pepin an agent of Byzantium, but rather of arrogating to himself as pope the emperor's power to bestow the titles and to signify that Pepin was now the protector of the papacy and of the Roman population. Perhaps the title was even intended to imply that the Frankish king was the defender of all who professed the Roman faith.

Pepin acted promptly to fulfill his obligation toward the papacy. In spite of the reluctance of some of his nobles, he undertook two military campaigns against the Lombards in 755 and 756 to protect the territories claimed by the pope. During the first expedition he presented a document to Stephen which came to be known as the "Donation of Pepin" and which ordered the Lombards to restore certain territories lying roughly between Ravenna and Rome. In the eyes of the West, at least, this provided a legal basis for the papal states even though much of the territory included was actually Byzantine property. Pepin and Stephen were obviously little concerned with the rights of the emperor even though an embassy from Constantinople protested the action.

The events of 754–756 strengthened the bond between the papacy and the Carolingians. The Carolingians owed their crown to papal sanction, and the papal states, which were the key to papal independence, owed their legal existence to the king of the Franks. The popes had exchanged their Byzantine protectors for Frankish guardians and had profited in the exchange by laying claim to and taking possession of Byzantine territory. The alliance with the Franks was destined to determine papal policy for a long period in the future.

After 756, Pepin's policy in Italy was less incisive and vigorous. For the rest of his reign the popes begged him incessantly for more decisive intervention, but without success. By his failure to eliminate the Lombards as a factor in Italian affairs, Pepin left the popes in a dependent state. At the same time he was probably more deeply involved in the fate of Italy and the papacy than he realized, particularly as a result of his casual disposal of Byzantine lands and titles. In any case, there can be no doubt that his actions radically altered the role of the Carolingians. By using papal sanction to aid his exchange of status from that of royal servant to king, Pepin involved himself and his successors in the reform of the Frankish church on the Roman model, the protection of the papacy and its Italian territories. No other Western European dynasty could claim so extended or exalted a role.

Charlemagne, 768–814

It was Pepin's son, Charles the Great, who not only brought the Carolingian dynasty to its full glory but gave it its name. Following lines of policy already charted by Charles Martel and Pepin, Charlemagne achieved success in nearly every venture he undertook. Graced with a dynamic personality and great talent, he made a strong impression on all his contemporaries. His powerful physique, unbounded energy, personal courage, not to mention his love of hunting and the banquet hall, made him a natural leader of the Frankish warriors who constituted his chief support. His deep piety, expressing itself in constant attendance at religious services and in a genuine concern for the welfare of the church, endeared him to the clergy. By the standards of his day, Charles was well educated for a layman. He spoke and read Latin, an accomplishment which permitted him to enjoy the company of the scholars who gathered about him at his chief residence in Aachen.

Charles earned glory first as a conqueror. In the spring of almost every year of his reign he summoned his great nobles to a meeting at one of his residences. Each came armed and supplied for a campaign. After joining the clergy in whatever political deliberations the king proposed, the warriors set off for a campaign that usually lasted into the summer. Sometimes the nobles and their entourages were joined by infantry contingents of freemen mustered by royal officials. Charles himself often led these expeditions, but on occasion, especially when more than one army had to be sent out, he would entrust commands to faithful vassals. The success of these repeated campaigns expanded the Frankish kingdom into an empire embracing more territory than had been controlled by any single ruler in the west since the fall of Rome.

Charles's first decisive military venture was the victorious conclusion of the struggle his father had begun with the Lombards. Invading Italy in 773, he drove the Lombard army behind the walls of the royal capital at Pavia and after a long siege reduced them to capitulation. So complete was his victory that Charlemagne was able to depose the Lombard king, assume the crown himself, and annex all Lombard lands. This gave him control of all Italy except the Byzantine territories in the southern part of the peninsula, but he recognized the pope's authority in the territories assigned to him by the Donation of Pepin, and in return assumed the title of Patrician of the Romans.

Even before concluding this settlement in Italy, Charles

had in 772 undertaken his first campaign against the Saxons. These Germanic barbarians proved his most stubborn foe for over thirty years. Divided into small tribal principalities, the Saxons were no match for the Frankish armies in pitched battle. The Franks, however, found it extremely difficult to convert their military victories into effective control. Since there was no single Saxon ruler with whom they could reach a binding settlement, they were forced to leave small contingents behind to guard Frankish interests after each campaign. Against this form of restraint the savage natives regularly rebelled, slaughtering the small garrisons, and inevitably brought Charles back on another campaign of brutal repression. During one such campaign he slaughtered 4,500 Saxon captives in an attempt to avenge their treachery and to prove the folly of resisting the Franks. He also insisted that the Saxons accept Christianity as a token of submission and on more than one occasion herded them together for forced baptism. Charles also resorted to a policy of forcibly resettling large numbers of Saxons in various parts of the Frankish kingdom. In the course of their struggles with the Franks the Saxons had enlisted the support of the Frisians, another Germanic people living along the North Sea coast from the Rhine to the Weser rivers, making it necessary for Charles to conquer them too as a part of his final destruction of the Saxons.

In the intervals between Saxon campaigns Charles sought to expand the Frankish frontiers toward the southeast and the southwest. His target in the southeast was the Avar Empire lying astride the Danube. This nomadic warrior people of Asian origin had, during the seventh and eighth centuries, created a large state by conquering many weak Slavic tribes. Their raids in search of booty constantly menaced the Frankish state and finally provoked Charlemagne to counterattack. A preliminary expedition in 791 was followed by a full-scale campaign against the Avars in 796, which captured their great fortified camp near the mouth of the Theiss River, seized a vast accumulation of booty, and destroyed their military power, allowing Charlemagne to annex territory along the Danube.

In 778, Charlemagne led an army across the Pyrenees into Moslem Spain. This first campaign resulted in a series of defeats, climaxed by the destruction of the Frankish rear guard in the pass of Roncesvalles in a battle immortalized in the mediaeval French epic *The Song of Roland.* However, Charles later returned to the attack and before his death had established Frankish power as far south as the Ebro River. Brittany, a land largely inhabited by Celtic peoples who had fled the British Isles during the Anglo-Saxon invasions of the fifth century and who had enjoyed virtual independence ever since, was also conquered and annexed to the Frankish realm.

In the midst of these numerous campaigns against foreign foes, Charles occasionally had to deal with serious separatist movements of non-Frankish elements within his kingdom. In Aquitaine, where a strong Gallo-Roman nobility still survived, a rebellion had to be suppressed by force in 769. But serious restlessness continued until in 781 Charles finally granted the areas limited autonomy as a separate kingdom under Frankish overlordship and placed his son Louis on the throne. The Bavarians also clashed with the Franks on several occasions but Charlemagne reduced their resistance by replacing the native duke with Frankish agents in 788.

The object of Charles's campaigns was never mere conquest of territory. Instead he regularly attempted to introduce strong political institutions which would make the conquered peoples truly his subjects. Although they were permitted to live under their old systems of law, they were usually governed by trusted Frankish counts and dukes who not only exercised the king's power but were responsible for guarding the exposed frontiers. Especially important in Charles's program for incorporating new territories was his insistence upon the Christianization of conquered peoples and the immediate institution of a church organization. As a result of these efforts Charles managed to convince most of his subjects that he was more than a greedy conqueror. Instead he was hailed as a champion who protected his Christian subjects from the grave peril posed by barbarians, pagans, and infidels and promoted the cause of God. Popes, poets, and nobles hailed him as "the strong right arm of God."

While expending an extraordinary amount of energy as leader of successful military ventures, Charles sought to improve the quality of the government he headed. In general, he did not attempt any revolutionary changes, but through constant legislation and careful supervision sought to infuse a new spirit into the administration of the kingdom his dynasty had seized from the Merovingians. His main concern was the establishment and maintenance of peace and order among his subjects. Charles was ruthless in his suppression of internal dissension, whether of Frankish or barbarian origin. Orderly life required rule according to law, and he made a strong effort to provide competent courts where all free men could find protection of their hereditary rights. To create a government capable of bringing peace and order to so vast an empire called for a loyal body of royal officials. It was no small task to select competent men from the ranks of the nobility and higher clergy, to instill in them a sense of responsibility, and to control them once they had been invested with power. Moreover, the decline of the money economy in the Carolingian state and the consequent reduction of the king's income greatly increased the difficulty. As a consequence of the disappearance of the royal revenues and the frequent failure of lines of communication within the empire, the counts and dukes who represented the king in the local areas could only be paid effectively in grants of land, with the inevitable risk that they would use these resources as a base for defying the king himself. To obviate this danger, Charles attempted to bind his officials with personal oaths of allegiance and to control them by *missi*, itinerant agents sent out from the royal court. He also issued a constant stream of instructions, called capitularies, to guide and define the activities of all his officials. In the strong and able hands of Charles, this cumbersome system not only worked amazingly well but succeeded in re-establishing the prestige of the monarchy as a civilized and useful institution.

Charles clearly recognized that Christianity was the strongest bond of unity in his diverse empire. This realization, reinforced by his great personal piety, led him to develop a strong religious policy with the support of the chief religious leaders of the period, especially the popes. So eager was he to save souls and to add new converts to the Christian camp that he sometimes resorted to what a contemporary called "baptism with the sword." With equal vigor he pressed forward with the reform of the Church begun by his father. The Roman liturgy continued to spread with royal support. On a few occasions he even took it upon himself to define dogma, especially in connection with the iconoclastic quarrel, and to instill in his subjects a deeper knowledge of Christian doctrine. Nowhere in Christendom did there appear to be a greater champion of the faith. Most Western Europeans would have agreed with the contemporary author who wrote, "fortunate is the people exalted by a prince and sustained by a preacher of the faith whose right hand brandishes the glove of triumph and whose lips sound the trumpet of the true faith." It is little wonder that he was often hailed as the "most Christian king" or the "new Constantine."

The indefatigable Charles further distinguished himself by the ardor with which he promoted the cultural life of his court and realm. His biographer Einhard says that he "most zealously cultivated the liberal arts, held those who taught them in great esteem and conferred great honors upon them." The king personally enjoyed reading. His favorite books included Augustine's *City of God*, the Bible, and some of the Latin classics. He apparently also admired the heroic tales of the ancient Germanic tribes; at least he was alleged to have ordered that these oral accounts be written down so that they might be preserved. Most of all, however, Charles delighted in the company of the scholars who were attracted to his palace school at Aachen. This group, drawn by Charles from all over Europe, was dominated by the great Alcuin, who had already established a reputation as a teacher and scholar in England before coming to Aachen. From Italy came the Lombard historian, Paul the Deacon, and the grammarian and poet, Peter of Pisa. One of the best classicists of the day, Theodolf, was a Visigoth from Spain. Several Franks joined the circle, the most distinguished being Angilbert and Einhard, whose biography of Charles supplies the best-known picture of his court. The main purpose of the school was to teach students recruited from among the sons of the Frankish nobles and destined for service in the royal court or high office in the church. But assembled scholars also found time to read classical authors, Scripture, and theology, to collect books, and to compose poems, histories, grammars, and religious expositions. In addition, they often joined the king and his close friends to discuss history, Christian dogma, poetry, astronomy, and rhetoric. This was, however, such an extraordinary and self-conscious form of conversation that each participant was given a name drawn from the literature of the past; Charles was David, Alcuin was Horace, and Angilbert was Homer. The scholars of the court school generated a notable revival of interest in and knowledge of Latin and patristic culture, and their spirit reached out across the kingdom and fell on the fertile soil of the Benedictine monasteries. Thus, before Charlemagne's death cultural subjects had again acquired a prestige and incited a passion in his realm that further encouraged contemporaries to think that all good things stemmed from the Carolingian dynasty.

Charles's great success made his next step seem logical and perhaps even necessary in the rise of the Carolingians. On Christmas Day, 800, Charles was in Rome to exercise his authority as Patrician of the Romans. While Charles was engaged in a campaign against the Saxons in 799, Pope Leo III fled to Charles to complain that his enemies had attacked him in the midst of a public procession through the streets of Rome and had tried to blind him and tear out his tongue. Leo asked Charles to settle the problem. Charles therefore journeyed to Rome. After deliberations with his advisers and with Leo he exonerated the pope of any blame in the affair and restored Leo to authority. The king then stayed on to celebrate Christmas by attending services in the most famous church in Christendom, the basilica of St. Peter. While the king was kneeling in prayer, prior to the celebration of the Christmas Mass, Leo III

placed on his head a crown and the assembled crowd
shouted three times, "Life and victory to the august Charles,
crowned by God, great and pacific emperor of the Romans." The pope then prostrated himself before Charles
and adored him.

The intent and import of the event of 800 still puzzles
historians. Certainly the coronation was in part the final
step in the efforts of the popes to attach themselves to the
Carolingians and seemed a kind of symbolic act of jubila-
tion, celebrating the wisdom of the papal choice of strong
protectors of civilization and the orthodox religion. After
Charlemagne had destroyed Lombard power and made
himself master of a large part of Italy, the title Patrician of
the Romans, granted by the papacy to Pepin and assumed
by Charlemagne, proved to be inadequate. It neither gave
the Frankish ruler clear legal basis for his protection of
the papacy in Rome nor defined the obligations of the
Frankish king to the popes. Popes had long been accustomed to conducting themselves in a political framework
controlled by an emperor with well-defined powers. With
the disappearance of Byzantine influence from most of
Italy in the eighth century, however, the papacy was left
without a functioning legal system within which to work.
The Frankish "Patrician" did not effectively take the legal
place of the Byzantine "emperor," and Leo III, after being brutally attacked by a Roman mob, seems to have con-
ceived the idea of making Charles emperor as the only
means of constituting an official power capable of pacify-
ing the city of Rome. The Carolingians, and especially
Charlemagne, had championed the papacy long enough
to seem worthy of such a role.

Some of Charles's contemporaries, and perhaps Charles
himself, tried to represent the coronation of 800 as solely

the responsibility of the papacy. Charles's biographer, Einhard, said that Charles so disliked the act of coronation that, even though it was a great feast day, he would never have gone to the church where he was crowned had he known what the pope intended to do. But this statement can hardly be accepted at face value. For one thing the coronation could not have occurred unless Charles wanted it, and for another it provided the only logical solution to many problems confronting him. His successful conquests made his existing designation of Patrician inadequate to his true situation. Especially troublesome was his role in Italy, where he was assuming the responsibilities, without the title, of emperor. Several of Charles's closest advisers, especially the great Anglo-Saxon scholar, Alcuin, insisted that their master deserved glorification for his work as warrior, religious leader, cultural patron, and legislator. Since most of these men were scholars cognizant of the Roman tradition, it seemed only fitting that their hero should enjoy a title elevating him to equality with the great rulers of Rome.

His religious work especially convinced his followers that he was the rightful heir to the great Christian emperors like Constantine, and Charles himself grew increasingly aware of the position of his state as a world power. He resented accepting a place secondary to that of the Byzantine emperors, who condescendingly addressed him as "son" in diplomatic exchanges, but who nevertheless failed to protect the papacy, perpetuated what to the Western Europeans were false doctrines, seldom won military victories, and demonstrated a penchant for intrigue unbecoming Christian princes. This feeling became more intense after 797, when a woman, Irene, deposed her son, blinded him, and assumed the imperial crown in Constantinople. Perhaps it seemed to Charlemagne necessary to rescue the imperial diadem from what many in the West judged to be the unworthy hands of Irene in much the same way that Pepin had rescued the royal crown from the unworthy Merovingians a generation earlier.

It would be hard to argue, therefore, that Charles did not want the imperial crown, although it is quite likely he did not want it at the time and under the circumstances in which he actually received it. He may have feared that his coronation by the pope implied the subordination of the imperial office to a religious dignitary whose position Charles never considered superior to his own. In his scheme of things he was God's most potent servant, charged with supervising papal conduct in the same fashion that he regulated other phases of religious life. Perhaps Charles also felt uneasy accepting the crown in Rome, far from his beloved palace at Aachen, from his trusted advisers, and from his Germanic followers. Most of all Charles was concerned over Byzantine reaction to his coronation, but if he hoped that by attributing the responsibility to the pope he could allay Byzantine suspicions he was sadly mistaken. His coronation was deeply resented in Constantinople, and not until 812 did the Byzantine emperors finally recognize Charlemagne's imperial title. Even this recognition was only momentary, for the Greeks refused to accept Charlemagne's Frankish successors as emperors.

Louis the Pious, 814–840

Charles's successor, Louis the Pious, is usually not ranked in the same company with his immediate predecessors. In view of the difficulties that began to plague the Carolingian empire during his reign, there is some justice in demoting him from the ranks of outstanding Carolingians. However, in the framework of an inquiry tracing the expanding prestige of the Carolingians, his reign is of great importance in defining the nature of the emperorship and the role of the emperor.

Under Charlemagne there was considerable confusion and uncertainty over the meaning of the imperial title. Was Charles the only true emperor or must he share the title with the ruler in Constantinople? Was the new empire to remain unified or could Charles divide it as was the Frankish custom? Did the new office bring its holder new powers or was the title merely an honor signifying little? Did the emperor owe his office to the papacy or could he receive it by other means? In the last years of his reign Charles seemed not to have any clear consistent view of the nature of his imperial position.

His son and successor Louis the Pious, however, attempted to answer these problems. He was firmly convinced that the bearer of the imperial title had a great responsibility to labor for the creation of a more Christian society; the empire recently created must be an *imperium Christianum* before it was anything else. Louis sought to embody this ideal in an intensified program of religious reform that occupied most of his energies during the early part of his reign. He launched his reform in a dramatic fashion immediately after his father's death by purging the court at Aachen. Several notables were forced to retire to monasteries as punishment for their lax morality. Louis' sisters, one of whom had borne illegitimate children fathered by Angilbert, the "Homer" of the court circle, were compelled to take the veil.

A puritanical Benedictine monk, Benedict of Aniane, was brought from Aquitaine and installed in a monastery near Aachen as Louis' chief adviser, replacing the more worldly churchmen and nobles that had surrounded Charlemagne. Under the inspiration of Benedict a series of laws were then promulgated touching on every aspect of religious life. Poets and artists filled their works with discussions and representations of themes that stressed religious responsibilities, the ultimate effect being that the empire was "holy" above all things and that the most desirable quality of the emperor was "piety." Louis' religious sentiments were so powerful that he allowed the papacy to assume the role of grantor of the imperial office. Louis had already been crowned emperor in 813, when his father summoned an assembly of notables to Aachen and in their presence imposed the imperial crown on his son with his own hands and without the assistance of the clergy. But in 816 the pope came to Louis' court and anointed him in a ceremony which implied that papal sanctification alone gave substance to the imperial crown and that the empire was Roman in its origin. Louis' most important act toward defining the nature of the empire came a year later when he issued a document regulating the disposition of his empire among his three sons. His decree provided that one would be called "emperor" and would receive the largest portion of the imperial territory, while the other two would receive the title of "king" and smaller portions of territory. To assure the unity of the empire, however, the holder of the imperial title was granted supremacy over the kings, who would rule their allotted principalities under his general supervision.

Louis' attempt to define with greater clarity the nature of imperial office obviously exalted the Frankish ruler in the eyes of those who sympathized with him. As will be seen later, Louis' concept of empire was too exalted for the resources he commanded and for the sentiments of the society he directed. And so during his reign the Carolingian empire was constantly threatened with catastrophe. Nevertheless, Louis represented the Carolingian dynasty at the peak of its power and prestige. His title, "Emperor Augustus by the ordinance of divine providence," symbolized a degree of power far excelling the rank held by his family in the seventh century, when the Carolingians were merely rich nobles in the kingdom of Austrasia. Western Europe had at last produced a dynasty whose fame was widely known. For the moment at least the West had emerged from the shadows.

Nature of Carolingian Society

Merely to relate the success of the Carolingians by no means does justice to the dynasty's role in history, for it represents that moment when at least the ruling elements became fully aware of the fact that Western Europe had been launched on its own destiny. Carolingian history, therefore, is more than a record of events falling between two dates; it is the story of the genesis of a conscious and unique state of mind in the West. And yet the persistence of Germanic institutions and influences were so obvious as to raise doubts about the existence of an independent Carolingian society, standing distinctly apart from the earlier Germanic peoples of the West. Germanic law, for example, remained dominant in spite of the extensive legislation of the Carolingian kings, and almost no changes were made in the Germanic form of government inherited from the Merovingians. The Carolingian princes were all warriors in much the same sense that the old tribal chiefs had been. Even Charlemagne in 806 divided his empire in the manner of family property among his three sons living at that time, thereby throwing doubt on the seriousness with which he accepted the implications of the imperial title of 800. The Carolingians depended in the main on the support of the great noble families of Austrasia, assuring the predominance of a Germanic aristocracy in Carolingian society. The few insights that one can gain into the manner of living characteristic of the Carolingian age suggest the persistence of barbarism, violence, ignorance, and superstition. For all the revival of Latin learning there is clear evidence that the Germanic language prevailed over a considerable area of the empire and that the development of a barbarized Latin—the romance languages—begun in pre-Carolingian times and used by people in the daily conduct of life proceeded unhindered in its remaining parts.

Although evidence of this kind tends to suggest that the Carolingian era merely marked a continuation of the Germanization of the West, the survival and even the development of pronounced Germanic qualities provided a unique element in Western Europe's progress toward the creation of an independent civilization. But the mere persistence of Germanic traits does not account for all the new features that emerged to divide the West even more distinctly from the rest of the world.

Nowhere was this clearer than in political development. If Carolingian government differed little in outward form from early Germanic regimes, especially the Merovingian, it did have its own distinctive features. Perhaps most important was the clarification of the political alliance between kings and landed nobles which stemmed from the embryonic feudal order of the Merovingian period. Under the Carolingian princes, government depended largely upon the performance of services by men bound to the king by oaths of obedience and by grants of land. In this reciprocal system the land enabled its recipient to render the services to which he was obligated by his oath. The various instrumentalities regulating and defining this lord-vassal relationship were given sharper legal definition during the Carolingian era. Not only did Charlemagne himself devote much of his political efforts to the systematic exaction of services owed him by his noble vassals, but all of the Carolingians sought, on the whole successfully at least to 840, to convince their vassals that everyone's good lay in mutual service. In the pursuit of this policy they insisted that oaths of fealty be sanctioned by religion, bestowed liberal grants of land, provided impressively bold leadership in war, meted out vigorous punishment for disloyalty or rebellion, consulted constantly with the great men of the realm, and imposed speedy justice on wrongdoers. But in no way did even the most successful implementation of this policy impede the solidification of feudal institutions as a political system peculiar to Western Europe. This system of government stood in sharp contrast to the centralized, bureaucratic governments of Byzantium and the Moslem Empire.

Perhaps the ability of Carolingian rulers to utilize these basic feudal relationships for their own benefit and to persuade the powerful landed nobles to support them depended on a renewed awareness of the purpose of the state and the ruler which clearly manifested itself in this period. The early Germanic kingdoms, including the Merovingian Frankish state, had suffered seriously from the view, shared by rulers and ruled alike, that government was nothing more than a device for personal gain. The true greatness of the Carolingians derived largely from the fact that they transcended this corrosive concept of power.

In the Christian religion the Carolingians also began to

find a new sense of direction for their energies as rulers. Spelled out simply, they felt a compulsion to guide their subjects to eternal salvation, to shape here on earth a community of the faithful where good would prevail, to create an earthly city of God. Charlemagne seems at times to have considered himself a superpriest ordained by God to survey every aspect of life and to "correct" it in terms of his understanding of Christianity. This theocratic impulse prompted him to order popes, bishops, and abbots to amend their lives, to correct clerical abuses, to define theology, to direct the use of ecclesiastical wealth, and to supplement church funds with grants from the royal treasury. In addition many of his secular political actions—war, suppression of rebellion, administration of justice, patronage of learning—were directed toward religious ends. Thus in a brief span of time a new concept of the good prince developed in Western Europe. Far more refined than earlier Germanic concepts and far different from the Roman idea of the perfect ruler, this Carolingian ideal of the Christian prince long influenced political life in Western Europe. It is not to be wondered at that Charlemagne was glorified in legend throughout the Middle Ages; his earnest and vigorous service to the ideal of the Christian prince so impressed his age that he became the image of the perfect ruler.

The elevation of Charlemagne to the rank of emperor in 800 was the dramatic expression of the new political independence of the West and of the consciousness of many western Christians of the excellence of their Christian prince. Believing him truly worthy of his new title, many of Charles's advisers expected his Christian leadership to be even more effective after he became emperor. Even though they fully realized that neither the extent nor character of his rule could properly be compared with those of the earlier Roman emperors, they still thought him worthy of the imperial dignity because of his great service to God. Alcuin, the most influential scholar of Charlemagne's day, expressed the sentiment of many pious men when in 799 he wrote a letter to Charlemagne summarizing the world situation. He pointed out that up to that moment three dignitaries had stood at the head of the world: pope, Byzantine emperor, and Frankish king. Now two of the dignitaries had come on evil days; the pope had been beaten by a street mob in Rome, and a woman had usurped the imperial crown. Then Alcuin continued:

Now in the third place is the royal dignity which our Lord Jesus Christ has reserved to you so that you might govern the Christian people. This dignity surpasses the other two in power; it excels them in wisdom, and exceeds them in regnal dignity. It is now on you alone that rests the support of the churches of Christ, on you alone that depends their safety; on you, avenger of crimes, guide to those who err, consoler of the afflicted, exalter of the good.[1]

Once having acquired the imperial title, Charles and especially his son Louis took special pains to give it meaning that accentuated its Frankish and Western character. Neither really sought to realize the universal power over the whole civilized world implied in their new title of Roman emperor. They claimed no more than coequality with the emperor in Constantinople and the right to rule their own western domain according to their own peculiar needs and views. Both rulers sought to give expression to the political realities of the era, to acknowledge and act on the fact

[1] Alcuin, *Epist.*, #174, ed. E. Dümmler, in *Monumenta Germaniae Historica, Epistolae*, IV (Berlin, 1895), 288; tr. by the author.

that new, unique political institutions and ideals had emerged in Western Europe.

Religious development further reinforced political evolution in this early Carolingian period by increasing the differences separating the West from the rest of the Christian world. The rapid consolidation of Roman Christianity was the most significant product of Carolingian reliance on and support of the bishop of Rome. It was this intimate union between the papacy and the Carolingians which made possible the realization of Gregory the Great's dream of a religious community directed from Rome. The popes gained possession of a sizable papal state in Italy and the protection of the strongest princes in the west, laying the true basis for their independence. The Carolingian rulers in their role as religious reformers worked to institute Roman usages in liturgy and discipline throughout their vast realm, the result being that a considerable degree of religious uniformity was effected by the beginning of the ninth century. The widespread adoption of the Benedictine rule as a guide for monastic life in the Carolingian Empire resulted in a growth in the numbers of "soldiers of Christ" bent on propagating Roman usages and ideas. The close co-operation practiced by the Carolingians and the popes in missionary work resulted in the widespread acceptance of Roman guidance in matters of dogma, ecclesiastical organization, and discipline, as well as of Carolingian authority. In providing the Carolingians first with a royal title and then with an imperial crown, the papacy not only played a new role but achieved a new and exalted position for itself as well as for its proteges. These developments all meant that during the early Carolingian era Roman Christianity became an effective force over most of Western Europe instead of only in parts of Italy and in a few missionary areas on the fringe of Christendom, as had previously been the case.

The cultural revival nurtured by Charles, which has come to be known as the Carolingian renaissance, also served to accentuate in the minds of Western Europeans the concept of an independent Christian West. Believing that sound political administration, effective moral reform, and the purification of religious services depended upon the existence of an educated class, the king promoted cultural revival to serve practical ends. To achieve these goals the new learning emphasized specific forms suited to the needs of the West: mastery of Latin, the production of an increased number of books, the development of a usable style of handwriting, a careful study of Scripture, of the works of the church fathers and of selected classical authors, and a system of patronage allowing scholars to pursue these ends. Charles made his court at Aachen the center of learning, and he also encouraged monasteries to continue their cultural activity. Learned men recruited from all over Europe found adequate patronage to enable them to devote their lives to mastering the Latin tongue, compiling grammars, copying books in a beautiful new script, composing manuals for religious education, occasionally writing an original literary work dealing with theology, history, or biography, and corresponding with other learned men.

The emphasis on education and learning was accompanied by a revival of the arts which bore a Western European stamp. Church building commanded the best efforts of the period. In general, Carolingian churches were modeled after Roman basilicas of the late classical period. The basic ground plan consisted of a long nave crossed by a transept and ending in a circular apse where the choir and the altar were located. Side aisles usually flanked the nave.

Some churches, including Charles's chapel at Aachen, were built in an octagonal form, a style derived from Byzantine models. The walls of the churches were of stone, either cut into blocks or broken and set in mortar. Wooden roofs were used, since most Carolingian craftsmen apparently lacked the skill to construct stone roofs. The outsides of the churches were undecorated, but inside frescoes portraying scriptural stories adorned the walls. On the altars were golden chalices and candelabra, beautifully handwritten missals bound with carved ivory covers, and fine altar cloths. Although Carolingian churches in the main imitated earlier styles in their basic features, there were innovations of great significance for the future of Western European artistic history. Most important were the modifications made in church architecture to suit certain features of the Roman liturgy. Chapels devoted to the veneration of various saints began to be built around the apse. Crypts were constructed below the church as repositories for the relics of the patron saint of the church. The choir was steadily enlarged to accommodate the numerous participants in the celebration of Mass and the performance of the monastic offices. These developments were precursors of the Romanesque style that developed in full form by the eleventh century. In the delicate ivory carvings and the beautiful manuscript illuminations of the Carolingian period one can detect the prototypes for the magnificent stone sculpture which later adorned Romanesque churches. Many of the ivories and illuminations show a skillful combination of styles and themes derived from classical, Celtic, Germanic, and oriental sources, acquiring thereby a distinctive quality unique to the West.

The positive results of these activities seem modest if compared with contemporary cultural life in Islam or Byzantium. Carolingian scholars were familiar with only a few of the classical Roman authors, and their understanding of these was often superficial and naïve. The Latin employed by even their best authors was far inferior to classical models. Much of the poetry and theological writing was purely imitative in form and even content. For instance, Einhard patterned his biography of Charlemagne after the work of Suetonius, the biographer of the Roman emperors. In spite of the fact that several members of the court school strongly advocated a broad liberal education based on the study of rhetoric, dialectic, grammar, arithmetic, geometry, and theology, the actual operation of episcopal and monastic schools hardly achieved this end. Most of the students in these schools spent their time learning to read and write from rudimentary texts, answering questions posed by their masters about the symbolical meaning of scriptural passages, practising the various liturgical exercises connected with the performance of the divine office, and copying books. Even the mighty Charlemagne failed on occasion to excel in matters of learning. Einhard said of him that "he also tried to write, and kept tablets and blanks in bed under his pillow, so that during his leisure hours he might accustom his hand to form the letters; however he did not begin his efforts in time, but rather late in life, and therefore they met with ill success." Although the Carolingian period saw much greater artistic activity than the Merovingian age, still the total production of new buildings was slight compared with the late classical period or with later periods in the Middle Ages.

Yet at the time, the Carolingian renaissance, for all its limitations, had a tremendous impact. It made Western European society more aware of the importance of its cul-

tural heritage. No longer was learning the exclusive concern of a few isolated monks. Instead, it was again accepted
as necessary to the health of the government and the vigor
of the whole religious establishment, and as such, the responsibility of the entire community. Further the vigorous
concentration of Carolingian scholars on the Latin heritage
deepened the cultural gap separating the West from the
East. Not until many centuries later was the Greek aspect
of the classical heritage reintroduced into Western European hands. Finally, the Carolingian renaissance played a
significant role in creating the machinery of a productive
cultural life. The textbooks, the schools, the book collections, the methods of study and teaching, and the styles in
literature and art remained a permanent part of the Western European scene. From this Carolingian base most of
Western mediaeval culture was to develop.

Finally, in this brief inquiry into the outstanding qualities of Frankish society, a word must be said about the
fact that the Carolingian state truly became the center of
Western European society. Actually, there were many
political groups in Western Europe who were not a part
of the Carolingian realm, including the Moslem caliphate
and several small Christian states in Spain, the several English kingdoms, numerous Slavic principalities, the Scandinavian nations, and the Byzantine territories in southern
Italy. And still nearly all of these were to some degree
drawn into the orbit of Carolingian power, either in dependent alliance or dangerous hostility. When Byzantine
and Moslem rulers turned to the west, they usually saw
only the Carolingian rulers and thus tended to equate Western Europe with the Franks. It has already been noted that
the Carolingian state commanded the cultural talents of

all of Western Europe. In addition the Romanized religious order of the Carolingian Empire even reached out to touch some of the western Slavs and the Scandinavians, thus beginning the process of their assimilation into Western European society. As one observes the process by which "Carolingian" became "Western European" in the first half of the ninth century, he might rightly conclude that the most vital aspect of Carolingian history was the polarization of the entire West around an axis running from Rome to Aachen. This is but another way of saying that the Carolingian dynasty down to 840 sharply accentuated the unique features of emergent Western European society and did so with such a magnificent flair that all the world became conscious of its strength and vigor. This was the first Europe.

Moslem Power under the Early Abbasid Caliphs

While the great Carolingian princes were actively engaged in setting a distinct pattern for Western European civilization, changes equally important were developing in the vast Moslem empire which the Arab warriors of the Prophet had created during the course of the century that followed Mohammed's death in 632. During the first century, the impact of Islam on the civilized world had been chiefly military. By about 750 the conquering impulse had begun to wane; and as this happened the huge state that had been held together primarily by the arms of a small warrior minority underwent a grave internal crisis. After 750 the creative efforts in Moslem society were turned more toward constructing internal institutions intended to strengthen or preserve rather than further extend the empire.

The First Abbasids, 750–847, and the New Caliphate

The new developments in the Moslem empire after 750 were connected with the appearance of a new dynasty, the Abbasids, who held nominal power from 750 to 1258, but whose period of effective rule was confined to the years between 750 and 847. Successfully capitalizing on the discontent caused by the Umayyad policy of maintaining the Arabs as an elite within the Moslem empire, the Abbasid family seized power by force. Although the Arab warriors had assured military successes for a century, they came ultimately to be viewed as a parasite population living handsomely from the tribute levied on their victims. They offered little to their subjects, most of whom were culturally, economically, and politically their superiors. The Umayyad leaders were so preoccupied with war, diplomacy, and tribute-taking that they sometimes forgot that as caliphs they were religious leaders; and many Moslems charged them with the secularization and corruption of the true faith. As long as the Arab element predominated in the Moslem empire, the old tribal quarrels characteristic of the early desert society persisted. In this state of division and conflict, Umayyad rule was ripe for revolt and in 750 was swept away by a figure who claimed the incalculable superiority of direct descent from Mohammed.

This is not the place to chronicle the detailed history of the great Abbasid caliphs who reigned during the next century. A few of them, especially Harun-al-Rashid (786–809) and Al-Mamun (813–833), rank among the world's greatest rulers. Collectively the first caliphs followed a policy that revolutionized the existing empire and ultimately established the basic features of Moslem civilization. From the very beginning the dynasty insisted on stressing the religious nature of the caliphate. Charging that the Umayyads had debased the caliphate by making the office too secular, too much like the office of a Roman emperor, the Abbasids represented themselves as religious leaders charged by God to renew the regime of righteousness instituted by Mohammed. They began to demand that all Moslems obey them on this ground alone, and that the old tribal ties of the desert and the comradeship of the military camp be eliminated as the bases of political life. The Abbasids were "commanders of the faithful" but not exclusively commanders of the Arab warriors. They thus made their regime much more universal, causing the rights, privileges, and duties pertaining to the faithful Moslem to accrue equally to all who believed in God, not merely to an elite minority of Arabs.

In many ways the Abbasid concept of the state was a reflection of oriental ideas of priest-kings. It is not surprising then that the Abbasids moved their capital from Hellenized Damascus to Baghdad, where Persian influences were strong. The Umayyads had tried to pattern the practical institutions of government after Roman models; the Abbasids used Persian examples. The caliphs created at Baghdad an elaborate court, where they lived in splendid luxury in a withdrawn and mysterious atmosphere amidst their harems, their eunuchs, their courtiers, and their agents of government. Court life unfolded in one continuous round of ceremony, in which the caliph was the focus of attention of hundreds of brilliantly attired courtiers, each performing a ritual to the accompaniment of formal incantations and blasts of trumpets.

Although the personnel of the court was drawn from

the whole huge empire, Persians actually predominated. Even the armies of the Abbasid caliphs were manned chiefly by Persian troops. The court was distinguished by the existence of several well-defined administrative departments usually directed by a vizier, who was the chief agent of the caliph and often a figure of great power. From Baghdad an elaborate administrative network reached out to control provincial governors (emirs), who in turn created provincial capitals and courts modeled after Baghdad. The emirs developed a further hierarchy to carry authority down to a local level. Thus under Abbasid guidance a vast bureaucratic state replaced the old community of warriors.

The regime of the Abbasids also developed undesirable features: court intrigue, constant political assassination, spying, terroristic methods of political control. Yet it was a strong government when directed by capable caliphs, and its power was reflected in the magnificence of the capital —Baghdad—in the reigns of Harun-al-Rashid and some of his successors, as portrayed, for instance, in the famous *Arabian Nights' Entertainments, or A Thousand and One Nights*. Baghdad was a city of over a half-million people, second only to Constantinople in size. Its majestic mosques, ornate palaces and public buildings, bustling artisans' shops, paved streets, and public water system reflected the wealth that poured into the city from tribute and trade. The most splendid structure in the city was the caliph's residence, the Palace of the Golden Gate, whose towering dome dominated the city and the surrounding plain.

The upper classes lived in great splendor in residences bedecked with brilliant mosaics and decorative tiles. They adorned their persons with fine silks, rare perfumes, and precious jewels. Poets and artists found enthusiastic patronage among the rich of the city. For the scholars and students there was the famous House of Wisdom, a great university founded by the caliph Al-Mamun (813–833), with a huge library and remarkable laboratory facilities. Instruction was offered in almost every branch of knowledge by learned scholars from every corner of the empire. To the caliph's court, to the markets, and to the schools came a constant stream of travelers from far places to add a cosmopolitan air to the great city.

By contrast, Charlemagne's capital at Aachen was primitive. Its few thousand inhabitants, its modest church and palace, its handful of scholars struggling to master the rudiments of Latin and to instruct a few students in a simple course of studies, its lack of substantial trade and industry, and its domination by nobles who appeared at the city only when summoned to war indicate in part the superiority of the East over the West in the ninth century.

The newly constituted Abbasid regime did not attempt to continue its predecessor's campaigns of military conquest. In the west it tried to court Frankish support against the Spanish Moslems, who refused to recognize its authority. Harun-al-Rashid, for instance, caused considerable stir in Charlemagne's court when his ambassadors arrived in 801 and again in 807 bearing splendid gifts, including an elephant and a mechanical clock. This friendly attitude of the Baghdad caliphs relaxed Moslem pressure on Western Europe. Similarly, the sporadic campaigns waged against the Byzantine Empire tended increasingly to end in negotiated peace, and a well-defined boundary began to emerge across Asia Minor. As Byzantium was thus divided from Islam, each society could feel fairly secure behind the new frontier. The Moslems did wrest certain important territories from the Byzantine Empire during this period, the chief ones being Crete and Sicily, but they no longer ate up kingdoms and empires in whirlwind campaigns. This cessation of militant expansion relieved Byzantium of a terrible burden, and it introduced a degree of stability into the Mediterranean world that was not disturbed until the last half of the eleventh century and the beginning of the crusades.

During the first century of Abbasid rule, the Moslem world enjoyed remarkable prosperity. Having conquered some of the richest agricultural, commercial, and industrial centers in the world, the Moslems had then linked these economic centers in a common state, thereby easing the processes of economic interchange and encouraging the growth of trade in products and techniques. In order to increase the base for taxation the Abbasids encouraged trade and especially agriculture. Moslem products, especially Damascus steel, Cordovan leather, Persian rugs, Syrian glass, paper, and linen, cotton, and silk textiles were among the finest in the world. Agricultural methods were the most advanced then known. Western Europeans were amazed when they first encountered the variety of agricultural products produced in Spain or in Syria and the Holy Land; especially impressive to them were the fine livestock, sugar, and fruits. Because of this superiority numerous common words in our language derive from Moslem terms for the products of their shops and farms: muslin, alcohol, orange, lemon, damask, cotton, coffee, and sherbet.

Economic growth was further stimulated by the spread of a common language, which greatly facilitated travel and exchange. The ease with which residents in one part of the empire could learn about the living conditions of people in other far-distant parts of the empire bred new tastes and thus new demands for goods. The sum total of these forces produced a growth of trade, industry, and agriculture which brought the Moslem world to a level of prosperity as high as, or even higher than, that enjoyed any place in the contemporary world.

Universal Islam

The political and economic development of the early Abbasid period quite probably did not contribute as much to the formation of Moslem society as the rapid spread of Islam and the consequent creation of a vast religious community of the faithful. Even under the preceding dynasty many non-Arabs began to accept the religion of Mohammed, and, ironically, contributed to the fall of their rulers. Regularly treated as inferiors by the Umayyads, the non-Arab converts were ready to support the Abbasid challenge with its promise of equality for all Moslems and the unity of Islam. Under the new regime conversions to Islam continued to increase so that the population of the vast area stretching from Spain to India became predominantly Moslem.

Most of the conversions seem to have resulted chiefly from the appealing qualities of the Moslem religion. The Abbasid government seldom resorted to force as a means of conversion. Its usual policy was to extend considerable freedom to all religious groups within the empire and especially to Jews and Christians, who in the Moslem scheme of things were groups to whom God had revealed a part of the truth. The government did levy special taxes on non-Moslems and did keep them from holding certain offices, but these disabilities were probably not severe enough to compel conversions. The Moslem religion spread by virtue of its own merits, and it therefore became an effective bond of unity.

It is sometimes said that the century from 750 to 850

saw the definition of the orthodox Moslem religion that
has so long been a powerful force in history. Of course,
the basic shape of the religion had existed from the time
of Mohammed, whose revelations were set forth in the
Koran, compiled in the first few years after his death. In
the Abbasid age, theologians and canon lawyers devoted
a tremendous amount of energy to the study and elucida-
tion of the religious pronouncements (*hadiths*) attributed
to Mohammed when he was speaking as an individual but
not as the Prophet of God. Also the theologians and lawyers
labored to reconcile Moslem religious truths with foreign
religious and philosophical concepts circulating in the
Moslem world. The result of the study of religious tradition was the compilation of vast collections of material en-
larging upon and illuminating the Koran. The acceptance
of this tradition became obligatory on the orthodox, who
are usually referred to as Sunnite Moslems, and the over-
all effect was to transform into a complex and subtle religion the simple faith set forth in the Koran. The study of
law and the derivation of a code of conduct befitting true
believers were also pursued with vigor. Since there was
not an extensive amount of legislative material in the Koran,
Moslem jurisprudence became a highly speculative study.
The lawyers were forced to derive specific laws from general principles, a practice that led to divided opinion but
resulted in the elaboration of a vast body of law defining
Moslem rights and duties. This, too, became binding for
orthodox Moslems, adding still another level of complex-
ity to the simple faith proclaimed by Mohammed.

Neither the widespread conversions nor the definition
of orthodox dogma, ritual, and ethical codes assured complete religious unity in the Abbasid Empire. Large and
active communities of non-Moslems—Jews, Christians,

Zoroastrians—continued to exist within the empire; and by the mid-ninth century fundamental divisions had begun to emerge in the community of Islam. The main body of the Moslems, the Sunnites, were challenged by a vigorous schismatic sect, called the Shiites, who insisted that the essence of Islam was preserved by the descendants of Ali, Mohammed's son-in-law, rather than by the Umayyad and Abbasid caliphs, whom the Shiites viewed as usurpers. This sect tended to develop its own doctrines and usages, to split into internal factions, and to oppose the Sunnites. In spite of these religious divisions, however, the world of Islam found its major bond of unity in religion, and the early Abbasid period was the golden age of the true and universal faith.

Development of Moslem Culture

The spiritual unification of the Moslem world, fostered so strongly by religious developments, was also promoted by a vigorous cultural revival which permeated the entire empire. The first century of Abbasid history witnessed the real birth of a distinctive Moslem culture. The Arab warriors of the previous era had been little interested in cultural pursuits, and consequently cultural life under the Umayyads consisted chiefly of the continuation within their original habitats of the pre-Moslem cultural traditions—Graeco-Roman, Persian, Indian—with little interaction. The Umayyad period did witness the start of a cultural revival induced by the spread of a common language and a common religion, but prior to 750 little came from this new development.

The brilliant cultural revival of the early Abbasid period, which was destined to influence the history of the whole world, was based primarily on the translation of a large body of Greek, Persian and Indian learning into Arabic, thus making this knowledge available to all Moslem scholars. The range of this material was tremendous—astronomy, mathematics, medicine, chemistry, geography, physics, philosophy, belles-lettres, ethics, and law. Among the scholarly translators—whose chief center was Baghdad—the most prominent were not Arabs but rather Syrians and Persians, who as Moslems had learned Arabic but whose culture was based on their native traditions. In the cosmopolitan world of the Abbasids their knowledge commanded patronage quite irrespective of their origins. The period also saw a rapid development of those kinds of learning particularly suited to scholarly pursuits, especially linguistics, logic, and grammar. Between 750 and 850 the activity of Moslem scholars resembled that of Carolingian scholars of the same period—it would even be proper to speak of an Abbasid renaissance comparable to the Carolingian renaissance—since both movements were engaged in searching out bases for their new learning in their earlier cultural traditions. Nothing, however, so impresses one with the vigor of the Abbasid renaissance as a comparison of the range of Moslem scholarship with that of the Carolingian schools and monasteries. The Carolingian effort to recover and master a few Latin works seems pitiful compared with the huge number of diverse scientific and philosophical works recaptured by the Moslems.

The early Abbasid period left behind little in the way of architecture and painting by which to judge progress in these fields. Unfortunately the great monuments of Baghdad have all been destroyed. What little evidence survives suggests the development of a composite art style made up of liberal borrowings from Graeco-Roman, Indian, Persian, and Egyptian models. The typical mosque might well feature the long colonnaded hall of Egypt, the horse-shoe arch and stucco exterior from Persia, and the Byzantine vaults supported by marble columns. The use of geometric designs and of mosaics was already character-istic of the decorative arts. Because of religious inhibitions against the representation of the human form, religious painting did not develop freely in the Moslem world, and yet a vigorous style of painting evolved in palace decora-tion and a remarkably beautiful one in manuscript illumina-tion. Evidence is clear, however, that the new vital art of the Abbasid period, like the contemporaneous scholarship, drew its chief strength from a synthesis of earlier sources and traditions.

Byzantium in the Iconoclastic Age, 741–843

The achievements of the Carolingian rulers and the Abbasid caliphs were hardly matched by the efforts of the Byzantine emperors of the last half of the eighth and the first half of the ninth centuries. As a consequence, Byzantium suffered a further decline in her position during this era. Her loss was not in territory, as it had been from Justinian's reign to the early eighth century, but mainly in prestige. The claim of her emperors to be the universal heads of the Roman-Christian world was challenged by the Carolingian counterclaim to the imperial title at least in the West. At the same time the Byzantine court found another powerful rival in the Moslem court at Baghdad. Byzantine cultural life was equaled if not outshone by the Moslem renaissance and even challenged by the Caro-lingian renaissance. In large part the relative decline of Byzantium resulted from a bitter religious quarrel that divided the population and sometimes paralyzed the im-perial government. However, between 741 and 843 Byzantine society did preserve a basic internal strength in its institutions and culture that prepared the way for a brilliant revival toward the middle of the ninth century, a recovery which quickly restored the empire to new prominence.

Iconoclasm, Politics, and Defense

The dominant issue of Byzantine history in the era extending from 741 to 843 was religious. From time to time, it is true, the internal situation was complicated by foreign attacks, especially from the Moslems and the Bulgars, which placed heavy burdens on the imperial government even if they seldom posed a threat to its existence. As a matter of fact, during the early part of the iconoclastic age, Byzantine forces were actually able to take the offensive against the Moslems and Bulgars. Leo III had turned back the great Moslem assault of 717–718 and had begun the liberation of Asia Minor. He also inaugurated internal reforms which strengthened the army, the peasantry, and the central administration, and left his empire relatively stronger at his death. His successor, Constantine V (741–775) exploited the new situation with great skill. He took advantage of Moslem weakness during the transition from the Umayyad to the Abbasid dynasty to recover the rest of Asia Minor. Simultaneously, after a long fight he managed to check Bulgar expansion in the Balkans.

These same forceful rulers, however, opened a deep wound in Byzantine society by bringing the iconoclastic quarrel into public view, particularly when Leo III decreed in 726 that his subjects must cease using icons, that is, statues, mosaics and painted images, in religious worship. The forces leading to this decision were complex. Almost from the beginning of Christian history, art objects had been used to embellish the liturgy in spite of continual protests that such practices would lead to idolatry. By the eighth century brilliantly colored statues and paintings had become a major means of expressing piety, and some of the faithful clearly experienced difficulty in distinguishing between these artistic representations and the deity being worshiped. Although the problem prevailed throughout Christendom, it was especially serious in the Byzantine Empire. Probably the terrible uncertainty imposed on the imperial population by the constant danger of invasion during the seventh century had driven many to place an excessive hope in the miraculous intervention of God in the daily affairs of life. Byzantine literature of that era contains countless references to images of Christ or the Virgin that spoke, cured the ill, quieted the storms, and helped the suffering faithful with a wide variety of assistance. Large numbers of people filled their homes and adorned their clothing with the miracle-working icons. They prayed to them, sang to them, burned candles to them, and in every way evidenced a conviction that the icons were in reality divine forces.

These excesses ultimately bred a reaction among the Byzantines. Opposition was especially strong in Anatolia in the eastern provinces of the Byzantine Empire, where powerful bishops protested on theological grounds and where the simple peasants, influenced in part perhaps by their close contact with Jews and Moslems, tended to be puritanical and less inclined to demand visual representations of their deity. That the opposition to icons centered in Anatolia suggests that strong eastern religious influences had penetrated the Byzantine Empire during the seventh and early eighth centuries along with Moslem soldiers. A Syrian by birth, Leo III had grown up with a deep personal aversion to icons, which seems to have been reinforced during the many years he spent in Anatolia as a military commander. Intricately involved in the question of the icons was the problem of the role of monasticism in Byzantine society. The monks, through the development and exploitation of a complex and ornate ritual, exercised a powerful hold over large elements of the population. The typical Byzantine monastery was filled with holy objects around which evolved elaborate ceremonies. As a result the monasteries received such extensive gifts from the faithful as to make them appear to rival the wealth and authority of the emperors themselves.

In the edict published in 726, Leo III forbade any further use of icons in religious services, undoubtedly hoping both to purify Byzantine religious life and eliminate the independent power of the monasteries. From the beginning there was strong resistance to the decree, especially from the monks and from the populace in Constantinople and the European provinces. Leo, however, stuck by his decision. Disregarding popular riots in Constantinople, he reissued his edict, deposed a patriarch who opposed the reform, replaced him with a pro-iconoclast, and took legal action against those who opposed his decree. His successors, Constantine V (741–775) and Leo IV (775–780), continued his policy. Constantine was especially ardent in the cause, ruthlessly stripping the churches of their splendid art works and persecuting their defenders, known as "iconodules." Although his measures established iconoclasts in high church offices, his policy by no means won the support of all his subjects. Under pressure of persecution the iconodules defined their position and elaborated an impressive theological defense. Especially serious was the papal resistance to iconoclasm, for it further exacerbated the quarrel between pope and emperor and was in part responsible for the papal decision to seek an alliance with the Franks. This agreement, as noted earlier, ended in the seizure by the popes and the Franks of considerable Byzantine territory in Italy.

After the uncompromising iconoclasm of Leo III, Constantine V, and Leo IV, the empire suffered the even more disturbing effects of a sudden reversal of policy. In 785, Leo IV's ten-year-old son, Constantine VI, became emperor, with his mother Irene as regent. Personally opposed to iconoclasm and able to count on the support of a powerful faction in the empire, Irene caused an ecumenical council to be held in 787 at Nicaea to order the restoration of the icons. The iconoclasts, now on the defensive, remained firm in their opposition to the new imperial policy, skillfully exploiting Irene's ambition to acquire the throne for herself as a supporting issue. By blinding and deposing her son Irene did succeed in seizing the throne in 797, but the price of her ambition was high. Many of her own subjects doubted that it was legal for a woman to occupy the throne, and her usurpation provided the excuse for the imperial coronation of Charlemagne in 800. Not until 812 did the Byzantine emperor openly admit the existence of a western emperor, but well before that it was clear that Byzantine prestige suffered a severe blow from the bold action of the Franks and the papacy. Under Irene's reign there was also a relaxation of frontier defenses and a consequent resumption of Moslem and Bulgar attacks under the command of their great rulers, Harun-al-Rashid and Krum, respectively.

Irene, who was overthrown in 802, left her immediate successors a legacy of court intrigue, external threats, and an empty treasury, difficulties which were soon compounded by a new imperial assault on the icons. In 813, Leo V, another military commander from Anatolia, assumed the purple. Influenced by his eastern background, encouraged by clergymen who still detested the use of icons, and inspired by a desire to emulate Leo III and Constantine V, the new emperor in 815 decreed a second abolition of the icons. This policy was continued by his successors, Michael II (820–829) and Theophilus (829–842). Although they all resorted to forceful methods to impose their policy, these emperors of the second phase of the iconoclastic struggle found opposition more violent and determined than ever. The populace in Constantinople and the western provinces were fervently devoted to their beloved icons and could not be persuaded to abandon them by imperial orders. The monks who led the iconodule opposition developed a skillful campaign which extended the quarrel to the issue of church-state relations and succeeded in casting doubt on the validity of the imperial claim of supremacy over the church. In support of this line Theodore, from the monastery of Studion, marshaled a powerful array of learned monks. In addition to theology, the iconodules also restorted to court intrigue to serve their cause. Against this resourceful attack, the emperors, able administrators and competent generals though they were, found it impracticable to enforce their religious policy.

Once again it was a woman's hand which ended the iconoclastic quarrel. After the death of Theophilus, his widow Theodora assumed the regency for her young son Michael III. Moved by a clear realization that the iconoclastic quarrel was both undermining imperial authority and losing its appeal, Theodora and her advisers began cautiously to restore the icons. At the same time the adherents of iconoclasm were treated with considerable moderation, to make their defeat easier to accept. This moderate policy angered the most zealous iconodules, especially the followers of Theodore of Studion, but they were effectively curbed by the imperial government and soon made to realize that they had no hope of dictating religious policy to the imperial government. The end of the iconoclastic quarrel opened a golden age in Byzantine history. It had, however, been a costly struggle, breeding bitter internal strife for over a century, paving the way for a loss of valuable lands in Italy, encouraging the pretensions of the Franks to the imperial crown, and weakening the defense of the imperial frontiers. Unquestionably the chief iconoclastic emperors were men of high principle and strong faith, determined to reform religious life in their empire, but the cost of their intransigence was high and reduced the status of their empire relative to those of the Abbasids and Carolingians.

Byzantine Civilization in the Iconoclastic Age

Byzantine history between 741 and 843 was not, however, completely dominated by the bitter fight about the icons. During this period the empire maintained and even developed its basic political and economic structure, a factor which assured a rapid recovery once the religious struggle was ended.

The great strength of the Byzantine political system derived from the emperor's claim to absolute power as God's agent on earth. Not one emperor from Leo III to Theophilus ever relaxed either his autocratic pretentions or the sense of responsibility for the welfare of his subjects implied in his exalted claims. Even the most ardent iconoclastic emperors, such as Leo III, Constantine V, and Theophilus, enjoyed high respect for their efforts to defend the empire and to render justice to their subjects. Theophilus, for instance, became a hero in the eyes of the population of Constantinople for his efforts in behalf of justice. He made frequent trips through the streets of the city to ask people the price of food and clothing, to punish those guilty of cheating, and to allow all who desired to approach him with their requests. The centralized bureaucracy operated efficiently in the service of the emperor and proved capable of sustaining the ordinary functions of government throughout the period. The emperors were keenly conscious of regulating the conduct of their numerous civil servants. Leo III, for instance, undertook an important revision of the Code of Justinian in order to provide a more usable guide for the actions of the imperial courts. This revised code, called the *Ecloga*, was written in Greek instead of Latin and represented a modernization of parts of Justinian's Code to fit the requirements of the new age.

At times the imperial government was impeded by lack of income, but again reforms were instituted to provide the resources needed for effective government. The sound financial system of the empire offers a marked contrast with the contemporary Carolingian state which had to rely on the personal services of royal vassals to conduct the affairs of state. The power of the emperor was effectively exercised through an efficient system of local government which enacted the will of the emperor in every corner of the empire.

Probably the chief source of imperial strength was the military system. The emperors of the iconoclastic era continued to utilize the system of recruitment and organization instituted during the seventh century, the bulk of the soldiers being drawn from the free peasantry to whom land was granted in return for military service. The theme organization was extended and refined to assure the efficient use of military resources. Even when the religious quarrels were fiercest, the emperors of the iconoclastic era could rely on the military forces to act vigorously and efficiently against external foes. Especially useful in supporting the efforts of the army was the well-organized Byzantine diplomatic corps, which operated far and wide—in the Moslem world, among the Slavs, in Bulgaria, and in the West—to gain allies and to frustrate enemies. In general, the bitter internal quarrels of the era did not seriously weaken the structure of Byzantine autocracy, although at times they did divert its energies into fruitless ventures.

Even during the iconoclastic struggle and in spite of the efforts of some—especially the monks—to free the church from imperial control, the church continued throughout this period to add its vigorous support to the power of the autocratic emperor. The patriarch of Constantinople was the head of the Byzantine church and usually conducted himself as an agent of the emperor who elected him. The bishops serving under the patriarch generally followed his guidance, creating a well-defined hierarchy that labored to encourage unity and obedience within the empire. The populace, always moved by strong religious sentiments, continued to be responsive to ecclesiastical leadership. This close intertwining of state and church, begun earlier in Byzantine history, continued virtually uninterrupted throughout the iconoclastic struggle. Although it would hardly have appeared so at the time, the violent strife probably deepened spiritual life in Byzantine society, particularly in monastic circles, by revealing excesses in some liturgical usages and by forcing Christians to think about the meaning of their religious practices. Iconoclasm also contributed significantly to the separation of the Byzantine church from the rest of the Christian community. Believing iconoclasm to be heretical, the popes bent their labors more toward preserving the purity of religious life in the West rather than the universal structure. When the iconoclastic struggle was finally ended, the papacy had already cemented its alliance with the Franks, making it impossible to resume relationships between Rome and Constantinople on the old basis. Similarly the patriarchs of Constantinople had benefitted from the widening breach by receiving clearer recognition as leaders of the Byzantine church. No schism yet existed between East and West, but each of these two segments of the Christian world had gained a firmer conviction of its own separate existence.

The imperial government was also solidly grounded in the economic bases of the country. Clearly recognizing the importance of the independent peasantry the emperors sought to improve their condition and to protect them against the encroachments of the aristocratic landowners. As part of the same over-all policy, traders and artisans were encouraged and favored in the empire. As a result, Constantinople remained one of the great trading and manufacturing centers of the world even after the Moslems had cut into this sphere by seizing control of strategic Mediterranean positions, especially Sicily and Crete. These losses were not severe enough to affect the basic vitality of the teeming markets and shops which continued to provide an array of products that contributed to the brilliance and comfort as well as the wealth of Byzantine society.

The iconoclastic period was not, however, one of great cultural brilliance. The religious dispute resulted in the widespread destruction of religious art. Many learned men were silenced by persecution, exile, and even martyrdom.

Some of the literature of the period was so violently partisan as to lose all value. And yet the iconoclastic dispute did have a stimulating effect that called forth important intellectual and artistic efforts which were to bear fruit ultimately in a splendid cultural revival. The religious conflict provoked an avid interest in theological studies. In their search for self-justification, scholars on both sides of the issue studied Scripture and the church fathers with a new intensity which not only increased concern with religion but indirectly stimulated interest in education. Study of the Greek classics honed men's skills in dialectic and rhetoric, as the extensive writings of John of Damascus (died about 750) and Theodore of Studion, both opponents of iconoclasm, illustrate. Theodore of Studion also played an important role in emphasizing internal discipline and learning in the monasteries, a reform that eventually produced several intellectual leaders destined to bring glory to Byzantine society after 850.

Even in art, where the iconoclastic quarrel had the most destructive influence, there were evidences of renewed vitality. Those most violently opposed to the pictorial representation of Christ, the Virgin, and the saints were not hostile to other kinds of art. As a consequence the artists cultivated new themes and expressed themselves with considerable skill in scenes of everyday life, portraiture, and historical subjects, revealing marked tendencies toward realism modeled on Hellenistic styles and abstraction derived from Moslem geometrical designs. One noted historian of Byzantine art has said that the iconoclastic period witnessed the sowing of artistic seeds which produced a golden harvest in the late ninth and tenth centuries, with the return to late classical models. This continuing vital tradition, based on an interest in classical culture and strongly influenced by religious ideals, gave to Byzantine intellectual and artistic life a special quality that accentuated its differentiation from Western European and Moslem civilizations.

During the century from 750 to 850 the Mediterranean world had thus passed through a new phase of its history. By 850 the three distinctive civilizations were much more firmly established in their different ways than had been the case in 750. Especially rapid had been the progress of Western Europeans in the articulation of their cultural, religious, and political life. The Moslems had supplemented their demonstrated military power by developing a Moslem culture and by transforming their faith into a truly universal religion. In spite of being weakened internally by almost constant religious quarrels, the Byzantine Empire had sustained its basic institutions and had kept its political, religious, and cultural identity. By 850 old Rome was almost lost from sight behind the three new societies which were already filling the stage of the Mediterranean world and beginning to experience the pressures and tensions of their new circumstances and relationships.

CHAPTER III

Internal Division within the New Civilization

ABOUT the middle of the ninth century, the Mediterranean area entered a third—and, for this study, final—phase of its evolution away from the unity of Rome toward tripartition into Moslem, Byzantine, and Western European civilizations. The distinctive feature of the century following approximately 850 is not to be found in any remarkable new departures from the already established characteristics of the three civilizations. Each continued to develop in its own particular direction, thus accentuating the course of historical growth that has been outlined in preceding parts of this essay. There was no undoing the effects of the rise of Islam or the Germanization of the West or the transformations of Byzantium under siege. The true significance of the years following 850 lies in an important turn of events *within* each of the three civilizations. The unity that had consistently been a feature of Byzantine civilization and that had come to be a near reality in Western European and Moslem societies under the early Carolingians and the early Abbasids gave way to diversity. Gradually the internal bonds of each of these very different civilizations relaxed, leaving loose groups of political units bound together by cultural and religious ties. Much of me- diaeval history is the record of the continued development of the individual parts which made up Islam, Byzantium, and Western Europe, and yet the bonds of unity, originat- ing for the most part prior to the tenth century, remained strong, making it necessary for the historian to continue to think in terms of Western European, Byzantine, and Mos- lem civilizations.

Fragmentation of the Moslem World

The driving force of Moslem history during the first century of Abbasid rule (750–850) had been a powerful universalism which strove to create political unity, to estab- lish religious conformity, and to assimilate diverse cultural heritages in a single civilization. During the century follow- ing 850, however, fissures began to appear in the Moslem political order which clearly warned of the emergence of independent, rival states. But while divisive forces were at work in this one aspect of the Islamic world, religious and cultural developments attained a degree of unity that was equally significant for future Moslem history. By the tenth century Islam had reached what was long to remain its characteristic form—a world of many states, often bitterly opposed to one another, in which individuals living at the far ends of three continents still found common bonds in religion and culture.

Political Disintegration

Even after the mid-ninth century the caliphs at Baghdad persisted in claiming the title of "commanders of the faith- ful," once the proud boast of the great Abbasids of the early period. But the highly centralized bureaucracy, efficient provincial administration, sound financial system, and capable military establishment declined rapidly after 850, with the decay and corruption of the central government at Baghdad and the establishment of independent political regimes in the far-flung provinces of the caliphate.

The integrity of the central government gradually succumbed to court intrigue, religious discontent, and the disloyalty of provincial governors. In this situation, the existing army recruited chiefly from Persia proved inadequate, failing notably to protect the caliphs against frequent plots and assassinations. Hoping to increase his security in his own capital, the eighth Abbasid, Al-Mutasim (833–842), introduced into Baghdad a troop of Turks as a palace guard. These Asian nomads, long a formidable foe of the empire along its northeastern frontier, had impressed the caliphs with their skill as warriors. Although theoretically slaves, they soon made the caliphs their prisoners, and puppets.

A few ninth-century caliphs sought to restrain the influence of the Turks. For instance, the same Al-Mutasim went so far as to move the government away from Baghdad temporarily to avoid a clash between his Turkish guard and the native population. But the caliphs were powerless before their greedy minions. The history of the Abbasid caliphate quickly devolved into a monotonous record of palace revolts, usually the handiwork of the palace guard but often originating in the intrigue of ambitious harem eunuchs, wives, or officials connected with the vast governmental machinery at the capital, and all having as their object the replacement of one caliph by another. By 945 an ambitious general actually led his war band into Baghdad in an attempt to capture the caliph. "The city of peace," sunk in incessant turmoil, was no longer capable of the proper conduct of the administrative work required to rule the huge empire. Successful military commanders were soon calling themselves "emir of emirs," indicating their effective superiority over the other servants of the caliph. In this deteriorating situation, the helpless caliphs were pushed into the background and encouraged to enjoy the luxuries for which the court at Baghdad became fabled. By the tenth century independent dynasties, first in North Africa and then in Spain, assumed the title of caliph, thus creating the spectacle of three rival claimants to the succession to the Prophet. The Abbasid caliphs, however, continued their shadowy existence as prisoners of various military cliques until 1258.

This disintegration of the Abbasid empire was hastened by widespread separatist movements which created numerous smaller Moslem states within the crumbling structure. The processes of partition were much too complicated to discuss in detail here; but the results were plain enough, particularly in the late ninth and early tenth centuries. As early as 756 an heir of the Umayyad dynasty had established an independent state in Spain which became so powerful and prosperous that in 929 its ruler claimed the exalted title of caliph. Two other states developed in North Africa in the ninth century, centering in Tunisia and Morocco. In Egypt a separate state was founded in 868 by a Turkish governor sent to that province by the caliph of Baghdad. Thereafter Egypt remained independent and became one of the chief centers of Moslem power, especially after the Fatimid dynasty, originating in North Africa and claiming the title of caliph by virtue of descent from Mohammed's daughter Fatima, seized power in 969. In Syria, Palestine, and Arabia there emerged a succession of petty states whose duration and power varied, turning the area into a kind of no man's land fought over by Cairo, Baghdad, and Constantinople, and ultimately Western Europe. In the eastern parts of the old Islamic Empire strong ethnic forces among Iranians, Indians, and Turks, and a growing impatience with Abbasid rule contributed to a comparable fragmentation, which produced a number of important independent states. Thus by the tenth century there was really no Moslem Empire; instead there were ten or twelve rival states competing with one another and evolving each in its own path.

This decay of Abbasid authority and the consequent division of the Moslem world opened the way for the intrusion of outsiders. By 850 the momentum of Moslem expansion had run down and Islam began to suffer from foreign aggression by the Turks in the ninth century (once within the Moslem Empire, they became Moslems), the Byzantine Empire in the tenth, and Western Europeans by the eleventh.

But this is not to say that 850 marked the end of Moslem influence on political life of the Mediterranean area in general and Western Europe in particular. The mediaeval Christian kingdoms in Spain arose out of a perpetual state of warfare between the Moslems and Christians, a struggle that affected most of Western Europe. Italian history was influenced by Moslem attacks from Tunisia on Sicily and southern Italy in the ninth century and by counterattacks made by the Italians and the Normans in the tenth and eleventh centuries. The intercourse of Christian Europeans and Moslems in Sicily and Spain, which resulted in the transmission of important cultural influences from the Moslem world to Western Europe, had no less significant impact than the earlier phase of conquest and political dominance.

Unifying Forces

While many forces operated to split the Moslem political world, there still remained the powerful unifying factors of religion and culture, which permeated the separate and often competing political members and bound them together in the transcendent experience of Islam.

Religious life in the Moslem Empire was not completely peaceful in the period following 850. Several belligerent separatist movements challenged the Sunnite orthodoxy of the Abbasids, and religious differences were often encouraged by rebel political leaders seeking possible grounds for rejecting Abbasid overlordship. Especially active were the various Shiite groups which insisted that the true faith had been transmitted by the Prophet through a line of religious leaders descending from Ali, Mohammed's son-in-law. Other movements, stressing asceticism and mysticism, were as widespread as the Shiite sects, if less aggressive.

And yet after admitting the importance of religious separatism, one must recognize that common religious beliefs still bound Moslems into a community. Sunnites, Shiites, ascetics, and mystics all shared basic doctrines, and all followed a fundamental set of laws and ritual practices. Their adherence to the Koran provided a common origin for their religious and political laws. Symbolic of the religious unity of the Moslem world from Spain to India was the daily ritual of bowing toward Mecca and repeating in the same language the same prayer to God. Diverse groups might argue and even spill blood over the intricacies of doctrine, but a single religion gave them a common outlook and a common pattern of behavior.

During the late ninth and tenth centuries important attempts were made by theologians and legal authorities to define the nature of Islam. From this period emerged some of the major official collections containing the sayings of Mohammed, expositions on the Koran, codifications of Moslem law, and treatises on theology which have continued to provide the bases of Islamic religion. The effort to define the true faith was an international undertaking, involving scholars from all corners of the Moslem world whose works circulated wherever there were believers in Allah.

A second powerful unifying force in the Moslem world was its common culture, which in the ninth, tenth, and eleventh centuries represented one of the major phases in the cultural history of the world. During the early Abbasid period, as has already been noted, the translation into Arabic of Greek, Persian, and Indian literature and learning provided Moslem scholars with a vast store of knowledge. Beginning about 850 they undertook to test this accumulated wisdom and information against the teachings of their religion, and they soon turned to synthesizing the diverse material in encyclopedic collections intended to summarize all knowledge by fields and topics. In the process, Moslem scholars frequently found themselves confronting problems which could be solved only by original contributions, thus diverting them from synthesizing and compiling toward truly creative activity. The results of these monumental studies spread throughout Islam, overriding political barriers and linking educated classes everywhere in common possession of the most up-to-date knowledge available in the contemporary world.

The range of Moslem scholarship during this period was immense. Theology and religious law commanded primary attention, but other fields of scholarship were also extremely active. In the realm of the natural sciences, Moslem scholars, building on their encyclopedic collections of ancient knowledge, created scientific manuals that were superior to any found elsewhere in the contemporary world. It is possible to detect in these works the origins of our modern scientific knowledge and spirit. The Moslems excelled particularly in medicine, where they supplemented knowledge borrowed from earlier societies by new medical discoveries. The great works of Al-Razi (865–925) and Ibn Sina (980–1037), known in Western Europe as Rhazes and Avicenna, respectively, were typical products of the combination of ancient knowledge and contemporary practical experience. Avicenna's great treatise on medicine was translated into Latin at the end of the twelfth century and remained the chief authority on the subject in the west until early modern times. Medical knowledge was put to practice in numerous hospitals built in nearly every important Moslem city, and at least in some cities the competence of prospective physicians was carefully tested before they were licensed to practice. In the fields of astronomy and chemistry also, Moslem scientists prepared huge summaries of past knowledge brought up-to-date by the addition of their own observations and experiments. The typical Moslem scholar in these fields usually combined astrology and alchemy with more legitimate scientific pursuits, and for many centuries everyone interested in occultism and magic found in Moslem scientific manuals a vast storehouse of material. Because of the ease of travel in the Moslem world, geographers were able to produce more accurate descriptions of the earth and its natural features than had ever been known. Mathematicians also made notable advances, in part because of their unique opportunity to combine Greek and Indian mathematics as a basis for their own. Algebra, invented by Al-Khwarizimi in the ninth century, was the chief contribution of the Moslem mathematicians, along with the Arabic system of numbering. Steadily perfected in succeeding centuries, these inventions ultimately passed to the West to form the basis for modern mathematics.

Although modern students are especially fascinated by the Moslem scientific achievement, they must not overlook the work of Moslem philosophers and its importance to later philosophical development. Many Arab scholars were captivated by Greek rationalism, particularly that of Aristotle, while others—mostly theologians who were drawn to mysticism rather than to rationalistic theology—found in Greek Neoplatonism an important source for their speculations. These and other Greek philosophers were quickly translated into Arabic. But the chief Moslem philosophers went beyond mere translation, seeking not only to reconcile the Platonic and Aristotelian traditions with each other, but to reconcile both with Moslem theology. This was a difficult task, demanding that the philosopher find a common ground between the revealed tenets of the Islamic faith and the complex logical abstractions of Greek philosophy without destroying either. The efforts of what we might call the Islamic scholastics reached a culmination in the extensive works of Ibn Sina, mentioned above, Al-Ghazzali (1058–1111), and the Spanish Moslem Ibn Rusd (1126–1198), known in the West as Averroës. These philosophers exerted an important influence on both Jewish and Christian theologian-philosophers, who were likewise seeking to reconcile their religious beliefs with Greek philosophy. Because of their own contributions and their influence on others, the Moslem philosophers occupy an important place in the history of philosophy.

The combined works of the Moslem theologians, lawyers, scientists, and philosophers (as well as a considerable number of poets, storytellers, and historians who have been unworthily excluded from this essay by lack of space) created a body of knowledge that united in a single cultural community men living far apart geographically. This vast array of knowledge, springing from numerous sources in past ages, was cast in a new mold by Moslem scholars in accord with the tenets of Islamic religion. In its new shape, this knowledge was able to serve as a common denominator among all thinking Moslems and as a justification of their claim to cultural equality with the rest of the world, and perhaps even cultural superiority. The vigor, comprehensiveness, and creativity of Moslem culture in the ninth, tenth, and eleventh centuries was marked, and coupled with a common religion it formed the enduring foundation of Moslem civilization.

This cultural achievement is especially important to a student of Western European history because of its impact on the revival of cultural life in the west. Beginning in the late eleventh and continuing through the twelfth and thirteenth centuries, western scholars appropriated huge amounts of Moslem scientific and philosophical knowledge to add to the meager existing store of culture derived chiefly from Latin sources. So strong was the impact of Moslem learning on Europe that historians say it contributed to a "twelfth-century renaissance." This essay is not the place to pursue that theme; but it is proper to remind the reader that the deep significance of ninth- and tenth-century Moslem cultural history lies not only in its role as a unifying force within the Moslem world, but also in its role as a civilizing force far beyond Moslem boundaries.

Byzantine Recovery

The Byzantine Empire, reversing its previous tendency to shrink in size and prestige, began about 850 to enjoy the rebirth of political power, religious solidarity, and cultural vitality which was to assure it a major role in the history of the Mediterranean for many centuries and to extend its influence into a considerable portion of the Slavic world. The primitive Slavs began to draw vital nourishment from Byzantium, especially in religion and culture, even though they successfully maintained their political and ethnic identity. Thus the Byzantine sphere of influence also acquired that element of diversity within unity which became characteristic of the Mediterranean civilization of the late ninth and tenth centuries.

Restoration of Political Power under the Macedonian Dynasty

In 843, as we have seen, the Byzantine government decreed a restoration of the icons in religious services, thereby ending the iconoclastic struggle that had so long divided the empire. The political recovery, which followed almost immediately and continued throughout the tenth and into the early eleventh century, produced a revival of such magnitude that it resulted in the golden age of Byzantine power. Its main architects were the rulers of the Macedonian dynasty which came to power in 867 and which included several of the most distinguished emperors in Byzantine history.

The first two of this line, Basil I (867–886) and Leo VI, the Wise (886–912), devoted their major efforts to redefining and strengthening the internal structure of Byzantine society. Seldom have two men differed more completely. Basil, though of peasant origin, left his home in Macedonia for Constantinople in early manhood. In the great capital he attracted the attention of Emperor Michael III because of his tremendous physical strength and his skill in taming horses. The close association of the two, spiced by an almost constant round of revelry, ended abruptly when Basil murdered Michael in 867 and seized the throne. Leo VI, on the other hand, was a highly educated and refined representative of the intellectual elite of the city.

Despite such dissimilar personalities, both Basil I and Leo VI worked vigorously toward the single goal of reconstituting a strong political regime. Their efforts resulted in an extensive body of legislation, the main import of which was to define anew both absolutist and divinely sanctioned monarchy. This legislation reached its culmination in the publication by Leo VI of the *Basilica*, a code of laws, written in Greek, which borrowed heavily from Justinian's now outmoded Latin code and improved upon the legal reforms undertaken in the eighth century by Leo III. Supplemented by numerous individual laws and descriptive manuals, this body of legislation served as a constitution for one of the most efficient governmental systems ever constructed. Under the Macedonians, Byzantine monarchy by divine right finally reached its apogee.

If the legislation of the early Macedonians defined absolutism, the rulers of the dynasty effectively put it into practice. From the time of Basil I through the reign of Basil II (976–1025), Byzantine government was a model of efficiency. The emperors were living personifications of the state. Basil II, though undoubtedly the most outstanding, was in many ways typical of the whole dynasty. A contemporary said of him that "he ruled not according to the written laws, but according to the unwritten law of his own spirit." A man of great energy, intelligence, and ambition, he spent his entire reign in ceaseless activity devoted to the personal direction of military, financial, and diplomatic affairs of the empire. The imperial court at Constantinople consisted of a huge staff of trained experts whose ranks, duties, and salaries were defined in minute detail. The rigid system of control imposed by this bureaucracy on Byzantine trade, industry, and agriculture assured the state of necessary resources in money and material and brought the empire renewed social stability and economic prosperity. The system of themes was further refined, and it continued to serve as an effective means of provincial administration and military recruitment. Byzantium's highly skilled diplomatic service not only exerted influence far beyond her frontiers but served as a model for the entire civilized world; and her military and naval power became increasingly important in the Mediterranean and in eastern Europe. This revitalized Byzantine government, of course, did not escape occasional threat by court intrigues, military revolts, and popular unrest. Especially difficult were the ambitious aristocratic landowners who struggled incessantly to deprive the peasants of their holdings, to create larger estates, and to defy the central government. Nevertheless, the Macedonian regime was unquestionably the strongest government in the whole Mediterranean area during the ninth, tenth, and early eleventh centuries, as well as one of the most successful examples of absolutism in all history.

Internal reorganization led to a revival of Byzantine influence in international affairs. At the end of the iconoclastic period, the diplomatic and military position of Byzantium was extremely precarious and it continued to remain so under the early Macedonians. The Moslems still exerted dangerous pressure on Sicily, Byzantine Italy, and Asia Minor, and the appearance of a Russian raiding party at the walls of Constantinople in 860 posed a threat from a new quarter. But the Bulgars presented the gravest danger, and Byzantine resources were devoted chiefly to countering their attacks. During the reign of the King Simeon (893–

927), Bulgar pressure reached a climax. This able king's determined efforts to create a Bulgar empire equal to that of Byzantium drastically reduced Byzantine influence in the Balkans and forced the imperial government to make humiliating concessions to the Bulgar ruler.

By the second quarter of the tenth century, however, Byzantium was ready for a counterattack. In the Balkan area Byzantine diplomacy and Bulgarian internal problems first neutralized Bulgarian power. In the process of isolating the Bulgars, Byzantium created an intricate network of diplomatic relations with Slavic principalities both in the Balkans and in Russia and with such nomadic warrior groups as the Hungarians (Magyars), Patzinaks, and Khazars. Maintaining peace in the Balkans through diplomacy, Byzantium launched a major military attack against the disintegrating Moslem Empire. Under the great emperor-generals Nicephorus Phocas (963–969) and John Tzimisces (969–976) a series of crusading campaigns re-established Byzantine power in northern Syria and Armenia. About the same time a revived Byzantine navy recaptured Crete and Cyprus, thus restoring Greek might in the eastern Mediterranean.

Having forced Islam to retreat in the east, the Byzantine government was free to dispose of the Bulgar threat. During the tenth century the Bulgar kingdom had been subtly drawn into the orbit of Byzantium by religious and cultural penetration. The Emperor Basil II, prompted by Bulgar interference in Byzantine affairs, finally settled the score with the Bulgars by conquering their kingdom and incorporating it in the empire as a province. His vigorous campaigns, which earned for him the name "Bulgar Slayer," not only removed an ancient enemy but also assured Byzantine dominance over the Slavic population in most of the Balkan

peninsula and in a large area extending northward and eastward through central Europe into Russia. During this same
period the Byzantine empire even managed to retain an
important foothold in southern Italy, although its major
military and diplomatic efforts were directed east and
north.

Thus by the time the Macedonian dynasty attained its
greatest power under Basil II, Byzantium had been restored to a position of world prominence exceeding that
achieved by any previous emperor since the reign of Justinian. The territorial extent of the empire had been increased considerably by the recapture of northern Syria,
Armenia, Bulgaria, Crete, and Cyprus. Byzantine might was
solidly grounded on a strong government, a prosperous
economy, and a stable social order, and, at least politically,
the life of Byzantium was assured for a long time to come.

Religious Development

The resolution of the iconoclastic struggle not only resulted in a political revival but also opened an era of religious revival in the Byzantine church. This renascence
produced three developments which must command our
attention: the widening rift between the patriarchs of Constantinople and the popes of Rome, which presaged the ultimate schism between Eastern and Western churches; the
continued accentuation of distinctive aspects of religious
practice and thought which set the Greek church apart
from other branches of Christianity; and the zealous efforts
of the Greek church to promote the strength of the Byzantine government, especially in terms of its influence outside the empire.

The clash between Rome and Constantinople engendered

by the iconoclastic quarrel appeared to have ended with the restoration of the icons. Although the papacy was not consulted by Theodora, still the imperial order of 843 vindicated the papal position and once again placed in power a party interested in peace with Rome. The prospects of concord thus seemed excellent at the middle of the ninth century, but shortly thereafter a new and especially bitter quarrel drove the two churches even farther apart.

Within the Byzantine church itself the iconoclastic quarrel had left a heritage of factionalism. A party of clergymen and monks, dedicated to the eradication of all traces of iconoclasm and to a greater degree of ecclesiastical independence from the imperial government, struggled against a more moderate faction which sought to conciliate religious differences and to co-operate with the civil authorities in unifying Byzantine society. The radical faction, dissatisfied with the usually moderate patriarchs chosen by the emperors, repeatedly invoked Rome's intervention. When the popes became involved, they inevitably justified their action on the grounds of their supreme authority over the universal church. The Byzantine government and most of the clergy did not deny this claim, but often rejected its application when papal decisions interfered with the interests of the Byzantine state and church.

The situation became critical in 858 when Patriarch Ignatius was deposed and replaced by Photius, a learned layman and civil servant of great ability. Photius and the imperial government both appealed to Rome to sanction the change of patriarchs. The pope at that moment was Nicholas I, who held an exalted view of papal power and who was extremely eager to assert his authority wherever possible. After protracted negotiations, he finally refused to recognize Photius' election and excommunicated the patriarch, actions which, needless to say, were acceptable neither to the imperial government nor to Photius.

Nicholas' condemnation of Photius was in large part dictated by the emergence of a new issue of vital concern to both Rome and Constantinople. Shortly after 860 the possibility of important missionary work suddenly developed in Moravia and Bulgaria, both of which had been partly included in the Roman ecclesiastical province of Illyricum until it was taken away by Emperor Leo III in 732. Nicholas, moved by his ideal of Rome's universal authority, entertained high hopes of directing the conversion of the Moravians and the Bulgars and of binding them to Rome, in spite of the obvious fact that the Byzantine Empire could not permit such a development among its most dangerous enemies. If Greek missionaries could convert the Moravians, Constantinople might establish an important ally in the rear of the dread Bulgars. And if they could convert the Bulgars, a basis might well be formed for more peaceful relations between that dangerous kingdom and the empire. In this vital matter the clear-sighted Photius moved quickly and between 861 and 864 established Greek missionary forces in both Moravia and Bulgaria. His successes deepened the hostility in Rome.

However, the Byzantine missionary victory was not complete. The Greek missionaries in Moravia soon encountered German rivals and sought papal help. The Bulgar king Boris, who was baptized in 864 by Greek clergymen, also turned to Rome, in the hope of gaining papal approval for a separate Bulgar patriarchate. Nicholas exerted every effort to capitalize on these appeals, and Photius fought back lest Byzantine interests be compromised. As the jurisdictional battle widened, the protagonists played increasingly on doctrinal and disciplinary differences between the Roman and Greek churches, each trying to persuade the new converts that their opponent was guilty of heresy in doctrine and usage.

In 867 a revolution deposed Photius and made Basil I emperor. Nicholas I died shortly thereafter. Basil and his new patriarch, the previously mentioned Ignatius, made a strong effort to resolve the quarrel with Rome in an effort to strengthen the new dynasty. The papacy agreed to reinstate Ignatius, but extracted from the reluctant Greeks a recognition of Rome's final jurisdiction in disputes within the Greek church. This victory was soured, however, by what appeared to be a voluntary reversion of Bulgaria to the jurisdiction of Constantinople. Seizing this opportunity, the Greeks allowed the Bulgars to establish their own independent archbishopric, thus increasing Byzantine religious influences and decreasing whatever chances the papacy might have had in Bulgaria.

In succeeding years the papacy sought to regain control of Bulgaria, and its opportunity seemed to have arrived with the death of Ignatius in 877. Basil I recalled Photius to the patriarchate and sought Rome's approval for the installation of a man previously condemned by both Basil and the pope. Pope John VIII was willing to negotiate, however, and at an important council in Constantinople in 879–880 his legates agreed to a settlement. Photius was recognized as the lawful patriarch, while Bulgaria was restored to Rome's jurisdiction. This agreement marked a pacification between Rome and Constantinople that endured for many years. The Greeks had honored Rome's claims to highest ecclesiastical authority by allowing the papacy to have an important part in deciding the suitability of Photius for the patriarchate and had satisfied Rome's claims on Bulgaria. In return, the Greek church gained clear recognition for the capable Photius, whose subsequent leadership greatly strengthened the internal structure of the Greek church.

Actually the Greeks gained considerably from the settlement. In spite of their admission of Rome's supremacy, the long quarrel had demonstrated that the imperial government could have its way in choosing patriarchs. The papacy could no longer count on a strong following in the Greek church to bring decisive pressure on the imperial government and its ecclesiastical officials. By skillful diplomacy, tact, and the careful mustering of public sentiment, the Greek government and church could vitiate Rome's control of Greek religious affairs even while admitting Rome's supremacy in principle. The return of Bulgaria to Roman jurisdiction cost the Greeks nothing, for the Bulgars refused to accept Rome's guidance. Perhaps Basil I and Photius realized that the Bulgars were already so powerfully attracted to Byzantine religion and culture that the chance of their accepting Rome's authority was small. In any case, after 880, the Bulgar church developed increasingly close communion with Constantinople at the expense of Rome. Considerable credit must go to Photius for the development of this policy of respectful conciliation toward Rome coupled with the systematic exploitation of each new opportunity to raise the prestige and strengthen the internal organization of the Greek church. The marked success of his policy may explain the violent abuse of this great patriarch by western church leaders in later years.

A long period of relative peace between Rome and Constantinople began with the agreement in 880. The papacy, deeply enmeshed in Italian politics and weakened by the feudal decentralization of ecclesiastical life in the west, was seldom able to interfere in Greek affairs. When, on occasion, discontented elements in Byzantium sought papal aid, the emperors and the patriarchs were usually able to prevent effective intervention without arousing papal ire. No violent dogmatic disputes challenged the authority of the patriarchs. The penetration of Byzantine religious influences among the Slavs of the Balkans, central Europe, and Russia put an indelible stamp on their various states and brought Slavic Christians to Byzantine monasteries, particularly the many communities on Mount Athos, to learn religion and letters from Greek teachers. The military victories of the emperors in the east restored active relationships between the patriarch of Constantinople and the patriarchs of the east. The total effect of these developments was to raise the prestige of the Byzantine church and its patriarchs, to confirm its independent status, and to develop in it a strong sense of leadership among the converts of the Slavic world and the "liberated" Christians in the east.

By the eleventh century, however, changing conditions again sharpened hostilities between Rome and Constantinople and eventually produced the schism that has lasted to the present. Although the story of the final break lies beyond the scope of this essay, it is surely worth noting that the revitalization of the Greek church during the Macedonian era contributed significantly to the ultimate division. Having grown accustomed to independent existence, to a position of high rank, and to a role of leadership, the Byzantine patriarchs felt no need to bend before the demands of the popes, who—particularly during the great reform movement of the eleventh century—became more insistent in their claims to supremacy and more vigorous in their condemnations of Greek religious usages and teachings.

The evolution of the Greek church during the Macedonian era contributed significantly to the growing divergency in the doctrines and practices of the eastern and western churches and marked a second phase of this development. The emperors and their able patriarchs defined clerical usage and encouraged a distinctive religious ethos within their empire. The quarrels between the Greek and Roman churches that developed during and after the schism emphasized chiefly variations in clerical marriage, the wording of the creed, fasting regulations, the order of worship in the Mass, and procedures for administering the sacraments. These outward variations, however, were symbolic of more basic differences in the spirit of the two churches. During the iconoclastic period the Byzantine church had been dominated by puritanical ideas, but after 850 the old Greek elements began to reappear in religious practices. Signs of this new development can be found in the elaborate Greek Orthodox ritual, the exquisite symbolism of Greek religious art, the glories of Greek church music, the intricacies of Greek Orthodox theology, the powerful role of monasticism in Greek religious life, and the concepts of piety exemplified by Greek religious festivals. It is probably safe to say that many of these unique features assumed something like their final form in the posticonoclastic era of the Macedonian dynasty. Certainly the experience of this era dispelled any hopes that the Roman church may have had at the end of the iconoclastic quarrel of imposing Roman usages throughout all Christendom, and it laid the basis for more vigorous disputes over religious practice in later periods.

The third notable stage of the evolution of the schism was the vigorous support by the Byzantine church of the expansion of the absolute power of the state. The original imperial concept of the church as an arm of the state, and of the emperor as a religious as well as a political leader, had been seriously challenged in the iconoclastic struggle, when the emperors attempted to impose a generally unpopular religious policy. Considerable segments of the Byzantine church resisted, and the end of the iconoclastic quarrel was in a sense a victory for the church over the state. During the Macedonian period the emperors regained command of the ecclesiastical hierarchy, but they used their authority with great circumspection, manifesting deep respect for the church, seldom interfering in doctrinal affairs. This policy was explicitly stated by one Macedonian emperor, who said, "I recognize two authorities in the world, priesthood and empire; the Creator of the world entrusted to the first the care of souls and to the second the control of men's bodies. Let neither authority be attacked, that the world may enjoy prosperity."

In reality, however, emperors did not need to coerce the church, for the chief religious figures of the ninth and tenth centuries felt a fervent responsibility for the welfare of the state. They bent every effort to guide the populace to obedient service of the emperor, who was exalted on all occasions as God's servant and whose absolute authority was vigorously defended. And they were especially eager to support Byzantine foreign policy. Greek missionaries regularly sought to bind their new converts to Constantinople and thus were largely responsible for the close ties uniting many Slavs to Byzantium. The complete union of church and state became final during the Macedonian period. Seldom in all history can one find a better example of a state church operating within its proper sphere to exalt the ruler and to inculcate the faithful with loyalty to the state. From the ninth century onward Byzantine church-state relations present a marked contrast with the bitter struggles between church and state which divided Western European society throughout much of the Middle Ages.

Cultural Renaissance

The resurgence of Byzantine society in the Macedonian period was further highlighted by a brilliant cultural revival. During the long era when Byzantium was under siege and torn by internal religious quarrels, the Byzantine world was able to guard its precious heritage of classical Greek culture and early Christian learning of Greek origins. With the resolution of religious quarrels and the revival of political vigor in the middle of the ninth century, however, scholars and artists drew inspiration from this ancient heritage to create perhaps the greatest phase of Byzantine culture.

Beginning in mid-ninth century this revival was marked especially by the intensification of scholarly activity at the university in Constantinople. Its curriculum was focused on a study of Greek classics, and its teachers included the best intellects of the day, led by the great patriarch Photius. The imperial government, always the chief patron of learning and art, produced some of the great scholars of the era from the ruling dynasty itself. Leo VI the Wise and Constantine VII were both learned men, distinguished scholars, and productive writers. The state supported the great school in the capital, where teachers were adequately paid and all students were accepted free of charge. An emphasis on classical learning, primarily literature, science, and philosophy, gave Byzantine culture of the Macedonian period a marked secular spirit, even though religious studies were avidly pursued in the great libraries of the monasteries.

Among the many manifestations of the Macedonian renaissance, probably the most typical consisted of encyclopedic compilations drawn from the vast literature of ancient Greece. Like their Moslem counterparts in the ninth, tenth, and eleventh centuries, Byzantine scholars compiled manuals on nearly every conceivable subject: law, public administration, military science, history, natural sciences, agriculture, medicine, court ceremony, saints' lives, ethics, linguistics, and diplomacy among many others. Such a list makes it obvious that the scholars were inspired by a desire to serve their society in practical matters. Such work required extensive libraries, and as a consequence the Macedonian period was distinguished by great collections, especially of classic Greek literature. The use of such material, of course, necessitated careful linguistic training. Since by the tenth century the Greek spoken in Byzantium differed considerably in pronunciation, vocabulary, and grammar from that of the classical authors, linguistic studies were revived to train students first to comprehend the ancient authors and then to imitate their literary style. Numerous commentaries were drawn up to elucidate ancient texts and to reconcile them with Christian teachings and experience, but many of these reflected a vein of humanism, sophistication, and secularism which reveals the deep impact of the ancient Greek authors on their explicators.

Although this golden age was not primarily creative, the impetus supplied by study and compilation carried over into more original work. A remarkable series of historians recorded the actions of past and current rulers. Numerous biographies were written, especially by monastic authors who specialized in lives of the saints. And the endless theological discussion often presented fresh interpretations of doctrine. Much of the large body of poetry produced in this period followed classical models, and in the tenth century a native Byzantine epic poetry emerged. But by far the most profound inspiration is to be found in the poems and hymns which express the intense personal emotions and deep piety of the religious revival.

It was also in this era that some of the chief stylistic features of Byzantine art were perfected. To their adaptation of classical line and form, the Byzantines added a taste and talent for rich ornament and striking color that transformed what began as a sterile imitation of Hellenistic models into an original and powerful style. The most representative monuments of the Macedonian period are the magnificent churches of Constantinople, their walls covered with mosaics and paintings which not only portray with startling realism the great dramatic episodes of Christian tradition but dazzle the beholder with glowing jewellike colors accented with gold and black. There was also a lively secular art, expressed chiefly in palaces and public buildings, and although less of this remains there is still enough to establish its distinctive qualities. Tenth-century Byzantine art and architecture were also much admired outside the empire. They were imitated in almost complete detail in Western Europe and the Slavic world and exerted in each an important influence on the development of artistic taste.

The Byzantine revival of the ninth and tenth centuries represented a cultural achievement far surpassing anything produced by the Carolingian renaissance and only equaled by the Moslem. Furthermore this Byzantine renaissance assured the survival of the ancient Greek heritage in its original form rather than in the Arabic or Latin versions by which it reached Islam or Western Christendom. Western European scholars of later periods, especially during the Renaissance, depended almost entirely on Byzantine learning to provide access to the Greek classics. At the same time the Byzantine renaissance marked a vital step in the long process of creating the unique Hellenized culture which was to flourish in and around Constantinople.

Byzantium and the Slavic World

Restored to the rank of a major power, Byzantium after 850 was able to create a new sphere of influence in a considerable portion of the Slavic world, which served to compensate for losses in Asia, Africa, and Western Europe during the preceding centuries and at the same time to change completely the destiny of the Slavs.

Byzantine influences penetrated the Slavic world on many levels. From the sixth century onward Slavic tribes crossed Byzantium's Balkan frontier and settled among Byzantine communities over much of the peninsula. The newcomers quickly adopted their neighbors' superior ways of life. Even the constant clash of arms between the two groups resulted in some useful cultural contact through the Byzantine policy of settling Slavic prisoners of war all over the empire. There was also a steady stream of diplomatic exchanges, in which Slavic princes journeyed to Constantinople and Byzantine legates and their retinues traveled to barbarian capitals. The pomp of the Byzantine court, the brilliance of Byzantine society, and the splendor of Constantinople almost inevitably inspired Slavic princes to emulate Byzantium in their primitive capitals. Byzantine diplomacy was often successful in bringing Slavic principalities into the imperial sphere of influence, thereby opening permanent channels of communication, along which the traders and the products of the empire moved to a large part of the Slavic world.

The chief bond between Byzantium and the Slavic world, however, was Christianity. The conversion of the Slavs involved a long process, which began when they first settled along the frontier of the late Roman empire. For a considerable period the Byzantine church made no concerted missionary effort, and the process of Christianization among the Slavs was very slow. Not until the middle of the ninth century was a more aggressive policy established under the patriarch Photius. His chief agents were the scholar-clergymen Cyril and Methodius, rightly called the "apostles of the Slavs," whom he sent to Moravia in 862 in answer to a request by a Moravian prince for missionary assistance. Cyril and Methodius bent their major efforts toward developing a Slavic liturgy and an instructional literature suitable for the Moravians. To achieve this end the missionaries adapted the Greek alphabet to the needs of a written Slavic language, thus flattering the Slavs and convincing them that they were acquiring their own version of Christianity. But more important, this linguistic development also made possible the transmission of the whole vast learning of Byzantium to the Slavs through their various languages. The missionary work of Cyril and Methodius was not permanent in Moravia, and by 885 their disciples were driven out by Germans propagating Roman Christianity. Finding a welcome refuge in Bulgaria, however, they pursued with great vigor the task of creating a Slavic Christianity and a Slavic culture, both derived from Byzantium.

The conversion of Bulgaria was begun in 864 with the baptism of the Bulgar ruler by Byzantine clergymen. For a brief period the Bulgars wavered between Roman and Greek Christianity, but ultimately were won to Constantinople by the Greek willingness to allow them considerable organizational independence, even including a Bulgar patriarch, and to approve their use of the new Slavic liturgy. The desire of the Bulgar rulers to strengthen Christianity led to considerable borrowing from Byzantium for nearly a century after their conversion. Numerous Greek religious writings were translated into Bulgarian and formed the starting point for a national literature. Byzantine models were used for monasteries built in Bulgaria, and even for such activities of the monks as the writing of saints' lives and devotional books. Most of the churches also were frank copies of Greek architecture and decorative art.

Byzantine influences also began to make important inroads into Russia in the Macedonian period. The empire had long had an interest in the various inhabitants of southern Russia, especially the Asiatic nomads who swept across this area from time to time. In 860 Constantinople was attacked by a people calling themselves the *Rhos* (whence came our word "Russian"). Who these people were is not entirely clear, but they may have had some connection with new principalities which emerged in Russia during the ninth century. It was at this time that the Swedes (known as Varangians in Russian history) established cities along the river routes connecting the Baltic with the Black Sea and Constantinople. Kiev soon became the most important of these, its rulers extending their authority over the surrounding Slavs to create a powerful principality. A lively relationship developed between Constantinople and Kiev. Sometimes this took the form of war, resulting in several attacks on Constantinople, and at other times the form of alliances which provided the emperors with powerful support against the Bulgars. There were always numerous commercial exchanges between Kiev and Constantinople, and on a few occasions Kievan princes and princesses visited Constantinople to view the wonders of the city and receive the honors of its emperors. Missionary parties from the empire also made their way into the principality of Kiev and won converts in spite of the strong Roman Christian influences which had penetrated Russia from Bulgaria, Moravia, and Western Europe. Finally, the conversion of Prince Vladimir to Greek Christianity and his marriage to Emperor Basil II's sister in 988 or 989 opened the way for the uninterrupted flow of cultural and religious influences of Byzantium northward into the heart of the Slavic world which was maintained and augmented by the organization of a Russian church in close alliance with the Byzantine hierarchy.

Examples of the rapid spread of Byzantine culture in the Slavic world are plentiful. Law codes were created by Slavic princes on Byzantine models. A considerable religious literature, translated from Greek, began to circulate in Slavic tongues. Churches were built and adorned in the Byzantine style. Monasticism took root among the Slavs. The courts of the native princes were modeled after the Sacred Palace in Constantinople, and the conduct of government followed Byzantine patterns. The manners of Byzantine society were aped by Slavic aristocracies. The eastern Slavs particularly made rapid progress in the ninth and tenth centuries under Byzantine influence, but the incipient Slavic states managed nonetheless to retain extensive independence. As a rule Byzantium did not attempt their political conquest, but rather was content to attach them to Byzantium as satellites incapable of breaking the magnetic pull of religion, art, and learning. This orientation toward the north was the final step in the evolution of the new Byzantine civilization.

Partition of the Carolingian Empire

In the ninth century Western Europe's dream of a Christian commonwealth ruled by a single emperor was shattered by the disintegration of the Carolingian empire into a series of successor states. So devastating was the collapse that even these broke up into political fragments, thus inaugurating feudal disorder in the West. The shock, however, was not great enough to sunder the unifying bonds of Roman Christianity and the Latin culture which had emerged from the Carolingian renaissance.

Emergence of the Western European Kingdoms

Evidences of weakness in the empire, by no means lacking toward the end of Charlemagne's reign, became ominous in the reign of Louis the Pious (814–840). This deeply religious and idealistic son of Charlemagne, as has already been noted, began his reign by trying to solidify the empire and to exalt the office of emperor. His chief support came from a diligent coterie of ecclesiastical and lay leaders who shared his belief in the need for a powerful Christian state and his conviction that it must be grounded in Christian idealism. The emperor and his supporters, however, failed to capture the imagination of his disparate subjects scattered across an empire stretching from Saxony to Rome and from Brittany to central Germany. Even though many had probably felt an identification with the great warrior and lawgiver Charlemagne, they now failed to understand what his less colorful son Louis, surrounded by priestly confidants, was trying to accomplish. The widespread indifference and even hostility to the dream of Louis the Pious was revealed the first time it encountered a serious issue.

The succession problem presented just such a test. The Carolingian ideal clearly demanded that the empire remain unified under a single ruler. But Germanic custom, which exercised a powerful influence in shaping the daily lives of the Carolingians and their subjects, dictated that a kingdom was only a piece of property and must, therefore, at the death of the king be divided among his sons. Louis himself wavered in his devotion to the principle of unity, torn by the compelling pull of custom reinforced by the ambitions of his sons and nobles. In 817 he pronounced in favor of imperial unity by issuing an edict which provided that his oldest son, Lothair, would inherit the imperial title and the largest portion of the empire. His two other sons were to be assigned small kingdoms within the empire and under the overlordship of Lothair. Almost from the beginning the younger sons intrigued for a more equitable division. The position of Lothair and his imperialist supporters was seriously compromised when Louis acquired a fourth son, born of a second wife, and tried to provide a patrimony for him in a new partition in 829. From 830 until his death in 840 Louis' government was paralyzed by a series of revolts prompted by his sons. Increasingly the nobles joined in these affairs because they found the royal contestants willing to buy their allegiance with grants of land.

Lothair did succeed his father as emperor in 840 and held that title until his death in 855, but Louis' two other surviving sons, Charles and Louis, revolted against their brother. After a bitter struggle they forced Lothair, in 843, to agree to the Treaty of Verdun, which assigned to Charles a large kingdom of the West Franks, embracing most of modern France, and gave Louis an equally sizable kingdom of the East Franks, lying east of the Rhine. Lothair retained a long strip of territory stretching from the mouth of the Rhine down its west bank and into Italy. He was conceded the imperial title, but its significance was almost wholly vitiated by the fact that the other two rulers were given virtual independence. In effect, three kingdoms had been carved out of the Carolingian empire.

For a few years after 843 the three brothers managed to maintain peaceful relations and to co-operate on the basis of mutual problems and interests. The church, long faithful to the ideal of Christian unity, worked hard to inspire the Carolingians with the spirit of co-operation. Each king, moreover, was troubled by internal rebellion and the savage attacks of new invaders. North African Moslems began to raid Italy, even entering Rome in 846, and the awesome Vikings from the shores of the North and Baltic seas sailed in larger and larger groups into the river valleys of Europe to spread terror and destruction by bold and sudden strikes which the kings could not contain.

Not even these common concerns, however, were sufficient to preserve the fraternal co-operation. In 855 Lothair died, dividing his elongated kingdom among three sons and thus creating three new kingdoms of Lorraine, Burgundy, and Italy alongside the existing kingdoms of the West Franks (France) and East Franks (Germany). One of his sons, Louis II (855–875), assumed the imperial title along with that of king of Italy. He devoted his energies mainly to a heroic defense of Italy against the Moslems, seldom looking across the Alps to the main body of the old empire. Perhaps he realized that nothing could be gained from that area, which was rapidly sinking into chaos. Charles the Bald, ruler of the West Franks, faced grave threats of rebellion from his nobles, who were abetted by his brother, Louis the German, and he was unsuccessful in attempts to curb the Viking invasions which were especially savage in the territory of the West Franks. Although Louis was able to invade Charles's kingdom on two occasions, he had almost as much difficulty with his own minions in the kingdom of the East Franks. Both Louis and Charles spent considerable energy trying to seize the territories of their nephews, the kings of Lorraine and Burgundy. They achieved partial success when they divided Lorraine in 870, but their victory was a costly one in terms of the concessions demanded by the nobles, concessions which could only hasten the disintegration of the empire.

After the death of the emperor Louis II in 875, Carolingian history was dominated by two equally disheartening tendencies. On the one hand, a few hardy adherents of the old imperial ideal, led by the papacy, conducted a futile search for a prince, preferably one of Carolingian descent, upon whose head the imperial crown might be placed. On the other, within each of the several Carolingian kingdoms there was a collapse of effective central government, which permitted powerful royal vassals to acquire virtual independence and ultimately encouraged them to elect as their kings men who seemed no better suited to the office than the last "do-nothing" Merovingians.

The papal quest for effective emperors was a failure. Each successive emperor after 875 had less influence on the whole empire than his predecessor; the last holder of the imperial title was nothing more than a petty Italian king whose power even in Italy was largely undermined by the growing strength of the Italian nobility. By 924 the Carolingian dream of Western Christendom as an effective political unit had vanished. Even the imperial throne was left vacant from 924 until 962, when the crown was assumed by Otto the Great, a German prince whose imperial domain embraced only the kingdom of the East Franks and that part of Italy lying roughly north of Rome. This general dissolution of unified political power was especially serious for the popes, who found themselves lacking a protector and threatened by the ambitions of the Roman nobles. In addition, Moslem raids continued in Italy, and the appearance of a new invading force, the Magyars (or Hungarians), deepened the political chaos.

North of the Alps, the Carolingian kingdoms disintegrated rapidly under the mounting pressure of Viking and Magyar raiders and the increasing independence of the great nobles. The Carolingian successors of Charles the Bald (died 877) and Louis the German (died 876) were incompetent and short-lived, devoting their limited talents mainly to schemes to deprive their relatives of territory. The Carolingian sense of responsibility for the administration of justice, promotion of religion, defense of the realm, and supervision of vassals had nearly vanished. The functions of government were increasingly usurped, or assumed by default, by powerful nobles, who made the traditional public offices hereditary, established the principle that royal grants of land were irrevocable, and in turn created their own circles of vassals. The principle of strong monarchy synonymous with earlier Carolingian rule was being undermined at a rapid rate.

For a brief period between 881 and 888 the Carolingian dynasty seemed destined to recover when Charles the Fat, son of Louis the German, was successively elected king of the East Franks, king of Italy, emperor, and finally king of the West Franks, thereby reuniting the whole empire under a single Carolingian ruler. But this was only a fortuitous interlude. Charles's early death in 888 resulted not only in the revival of the separatist trend of the preceding half century but also in widespread reaction against the Carolingians. Even before the death of Charles the Fat, the West Frankish nobles elected Eudo, count of Paris, as their king, his chief recommendation being his strong defense of

Paris against the Vikings. The Carolingian dynasty was later restored to the West Frankish throne and lasted until 987, but the election of 887 indicated that the hereditary right of the Carolingians to the throne was no longer admitted by the nobles and clergy. In the East Frankish kingdom the last ruler of Carolingian descent was Louis the Child; when he died in 911 the powerful East Frankish nobles and clergy elected the duke of Franconia, a non-Carolingian, as their king. In Italy, Provence, and Burgundy non-Carolingian kings were also elevated to the royal thrones.

And thus the heirs of Charlemagne dissipated their heritage. The imperial title created in 800 to unite Western Christians was by 900 held by a weak Italian king whose voice commanded little attention in Italy and none elsewhere. The empire had given place to the new nations of France, Germany, Italy, Burgundy, and Provence. Although these kingdoms were to bear the stamp of their Carolingian origin for many centuries, their emergence in the ninth century announced a new stage in European history.

To round out the picture of progressive political division of the West a word must be said here about the political fate of the rest of Western Europe. During the ninth century the world witnessed the grouping of Scandinavian war tribes into the three distinct kingdoms of Norway, Denmark, and Sweden. These turbulent realms, under the nominal rule of weak kings produced seemingly endless waves of Viking adventurers who attacked accessible parts of Western Europe, Russia, the British Isles, Iceland, Greenland, and perhaps even North America between the late eighth and the early tenth centuries. Many of the raiders ultimately settled in the lands they ravaged, among them

Norman France, northern England, Ireland, Iceland, and the regions of Novgorod and Kiev in Russia. In these far-flung places the Vikings rapidly established themselves and played vital roles in European history before they were absorbed by the local population. In spite of these emigrations the Scandinavian kingdoms continued to develop and increasingly took an important part in Europe's political development.

The ninth century was crucial in England's early history. Into the chaos of petty states founded by earlier Germanic conquerors, the Vikings launched a series of devastating raids that first resulted in the conquest and occupation of much of northern Britain and then produced a strong national reaction. The hero of this recovery was Alfred the Great (871–899), whose defense of Wessex in southern England saved his kingdom from the Vikings and earned for him the title of "founder" of England. His immediate successors led the forces of Wessex in a counterattack which reconquered northern England and created a unified English kingdom to join the other independent states emerging in Western Europe.

Toward Feudal Society

The collapse of the Carolingian empire represented much more than the division of Western Europe into independent kingdoms. It was, in fact, only the most spectacular manifestation of the fundamental change in the political, social, and economic structure of society which finally produced the feudal regime. Although by no means uniform throughout the West, the process of feudalization generally involved certain broad developments: the limitation of monarchical power, the personalization of political obligations, the identification of political power with landholding, the articulation of a warrior-ruler nobility controlling a dependent serf population, and the growth of the manorial regime. Each of these principal aspects of what was to become the feudal regime had appeared and taken root before, thereby making what happened in the ninth century only the final denouement of a long evolutionary process.

One marked characteristic of the deepening crisis of the ninth and tenth centuries was the progressive limitation of royal authority, both legally and practically, through the development of vassalage. Although the great Carolingians had surrounded themselves with a large number of men bound to them by special oaths of loyalty, they did not consider this arrangement a limitation of their sovereignty. While these "vassals," as such special supporters came to be called, were favored by the king and expected to serve him, they were still subject to public authority. During the reign of Louis the Pious a subtle change began to effect this situation. Royal vassals, abetted by churchmen seeking to influence governmental policy, began to insist on a more and more explicit definition of what the king owed them. Each harassed Carolingian was forced to accede to these demands to buttress his strength against competing Carolingians. Inexorably, monarchy assumed the nature of a contractural arrangement: vassals on one side claiming rights and admitting duties, and kings on the other side also possessing rights and acknowledging reciprocal responsibilities. With increasing boldness, vassals repudiated their oaths of allegiance to the king on the grounds that he had failed to meet his obligations to them. Such acts—which not so long before would have been regarded as a serious breach of duty—were often sanctioned by legal enactments and by custom. The king was no longer a sov··

ereign; he was now a lord, supported normally by those inhabitants of his kingdom who owed him personal allegiance but not necessarily by the growing number who had become vassals of other lords. The last Carolingian kings were so weak that they could provide little justice or security for their subjects, leaving the more vunerable with little choice but to pledge themselves to strong individuals in return for the promise of protection. Eventually these arrangements produced an intricate network of personal relationships between subjects and lords without significant reference to the king and his authority.

Thus monarchical power all but disappeared, and real political power gravitated rapidly into the hands of great landholders. Increasingly vassals demanded grants of land or offices from their lords to provide them with the means of fulfilling their obligations to him, a development already sanctioned by earlier Carolingian practice. Gradually such grants, or fiefs, as they were called, became virtually inalienable, especially after they were made hereditary in the late ninth century. As a result this process of granting fiefs to vassals badly depleted royal resources, particularly during the troubled period of the ninth century, when the kings, seeking desperately to win followers, even granted royal offices as hereditary fiefs. Those nobles able to exact large grants from the king usually subdivided them into lesser fiefs, thereby creating political entities independent of the monarch and dependent primarily upon themselves. Soon the right to political authority was claimed as a necessary prerogative of the vassal. All these factors contributed to the fragmentation of political power, the virtual destruction of a central public authority, and the further entrenchment of the landholding nobles.

The practical consequences of the development of vassalage and fiefs in the Carolingian empire nearly defy description. In general, each Carolingian successor state split into many virtually independent principalities, which often coincided with the administrative subdivisions of the old Carolingian empire. The counts and dukes, who were among the most important Carolingian officers, had been charged with exercising royal power in certain well-defined administrative districts and were usually given financial support by grants of land. From the king's point of view the success of this system depended upon the willingness of the vassal to respect the king's superior authority. The strong Carolingians commanded sufficient respect to make the system work, but by the mid-ninth century the situation had begun to change. The counts and dukes increasingly insisted on their rights as vassals, often giving those rights precedence over their duties as royal officials. They exacted from the king larger landholdings, from which they derived greater independent power. Most important of all, they began to treat the prerogatives of office—collecting taxes and fines, for instance—as a part of their fiefs to be used as personal income, and they insisted that both their land and their political functions were hereditary. The kings, carried along by developing custom and their increasing need for support, were unable to resist these demands. Thus, by the beginning of the tenth century the kingdoms of France, Germany, Italy, Burgundy, and Provence had split into clearly definable principalities which were to play an important role in the later history of each kingdom. Treated as private domains by the vassals who ruled them, these fiefs were virtually independent substates under the nominal overlordship of the king. Within each substate, moreover, the same process occurred, and the vassals of the counts and dukes arrogated to themselves, in turn, independent power over their smaller fiefs, just as their lords had done with their counties and duchies. Some lords were powerful enough to control their vassals, but most were not. In this process the concept of public authority nearly vanished, and political rights and duties could only be expressed in terms of the relations of lords and vassals to each other and the land.

And yet monarchy survived the atomization of public authority into private power. Since the only legal justification for the existence of great fiefs derived from the authority of the crown, the great dukes and counts, however little intention of respecting royal power they may have had, were always careful to elect a king. Accordingly, at the beginning of the tenth century, the fragmented society of Western Europe recognized kings whose only effective power derived from their rights as feudal lords. From 900 onward, much of Western European history is the story of how these kings used their basic feudal rights, buttressed by the surviving Carolingian tradition that the king was his subjects' leader in war and their guardian in matters of faith, to reconstitute strong monarchies—or to put it more accurately, strong feudal monarchies.

The transformation of the political order from centralized monarchy toward greater and greater dependence on personal relationships strongly influenced the social development of Western Europe. The number of men who could hold land and exercise political authority—that is, participate fully in feudal society—was small. Within the ranks of this elite of lords and vassals there rapidly developed a characteristic pattern of life deriving directly from the feudal system—fighting, governing, managing land, and retaining status among peers. The virtues proper to this life were carefully cultivated—bravery, loyalty, prowess in war, concentration on local concerns, and independence of action. Not until the tenth and eleventh centuries did this warrior-ruler nobility give conscious expression to its feudal ideals, but by 900 an aristocracy of lords and vassals had assumed effective leadership of Western Europe.

The fate of the vast bulk of the population was clearly settled by the new emphasis on landholding and localism which hastened the regime of large estates. With land the only source of wealth, the feudal nobles depended entirely on its successful exploitation for their power. Increasingly they concentrated on the development of the large, self-sufficient estates or manors that had been emerging since Roman times. By the end of the ninth century the important lord or vassal controlled many manors, with part of the land of each reserved to supply his needs. The rest of the land was divided into tenancies granted to peasants who paid for the use of their plots by returning produce to the lord and by assuming the burden of tilling the lord's portion of the manor. To assure the orderly operation of this system, the peasants for the most part were legally attached to the manors as serfs. Their political and social life was necessarily directed by the manorial lord, thus instituting the practice of private local government on each manor. Although the noble was complete master of the manor, his fortune depended upon the labor of his serfs, a fact which encouraged a paternalistic attitude toward the serf's welfare but which did not prevent the development of a distinct peasant social order. Even though the predominance of self-contained estates fragmented Europe economically as well as politically, and transformed it into a wholly agricultural society, the new manorial system did supply Europe's material needs and create a stable world where the weak found protection and the means of sustenance amidst the confusion of military and political anarchy.

Common Bonds in Western European Society

The disappearance of the strong Carolingian government in the ninth century not only disrupted the political unity of the empire, but also dissolved the ties linking Europe's peripheral areas to a Carolingian center. The emergent feudal order, the new invasions of Europe, and the failure of Carolingian idealism also threatened the religious and cultural ties linking Western Europeans together. Nevertheless, the religious and cultural development of the last half of the ninth and early tenth centuries did leave a residue of unifying forces that must be taken into account.

The last half of the ninth century saw a continuing development of Roman Christendom. The central theme in ecclesiastical history was a clearer definition of the church's claim to guide Western society. Under the leadership of the great Carolingian rulers, Roman doctrine, liturgy, and discipline had spread over most of the West, and the idea that service to Christian ends was the ultimate objective of society took deep root. This trend had exalted the Roman church, but it had also imposed certain restrictions on it. Charlemagne and Louis the Pious conducted themselves as virtual superpriests endowed with the right and duty to discipline clergymen, issue religious legislation, and dictate moral life, but after 840 the church asserted its independence more vigorously by taking advantage of the opportunity created by the decay of Carolingian authority. Many bishops intervened in the quarrels of the Carolingian family. They boldly compiled collections of church law which were intended to establish ecclesiastical discipline but which had the added effect of laying a claim of the clerical hierarchy to direct political activity. These laws increasingly guarded the right of the church to control its own property. Especially significant was the reinvigorated papal spirit of independence. On the basis of events in the reigns of Charlemagne and Louis the Pious, the popes assumed the right to bestow the imperial crown, and by the late ninth century they were choosing emperors. They worked actively to curb the family quarrels of the ruling dynasty and to censure kings for unbecoming conduct. Careful study of the careers of popes Nicholas I (858–867) or John VIII (872–882) reveals that they had reversed the situation existing under Charlemagne by making the priest the guardian of peace, order, and unity, and the king a servant of the church destined to labor for those ends. Even so, papal aspirations were rudely checked early in the tenth century when the rampant Italian nobles gained control of the papacy and turned it into a feudal prize, and by that time most bishops had become so deeply implicated in the feudal system that their interests were largely local and private.

The church, however, had won important victories for the principle of its independence from lay authority before the feudalization of society reduced the state to anarchy. Against the background of the ultimate dissolution of political order the church transformed its growing spirit of freedom into a more fruitful sense of responsibility for the fate of society, and this became the major force of unity in the West. The very spirit of church teaching centered around the brotherhood of those baptized in Christ, the obligation of all to pay homage to God, and the common fate of all men in the hereafter. The ability of the church to divorce itself from complete identification with the Carolingian dynasty after Carolingian rulers forgot about service to these ideals made it the single remaining institution symbolic of the common character of Western society. In this respect Western Christendom did not differ too much from the Moslem world; there too, common beliefs, practices, and ethical values still remained the signs of a community superimposed on a confusing array of political powers.

The church served as a unifying force in another important way during the late ninth century by continuing missionary efforts among those who lived on the periphery of Western Europe. In spite of all the troubles of the era, new converts were steadily being won in Scandinavia and among the Slavs living in eastern Europe. The successful missionaries, often Benedictine monks, spread Western usages and doctrines and thus forged a link between the new converts and the "old" world.

Latin culture, too, continued to function as a common bond during the last half of the ninth century; ironically, the Carolingian renaissance bore some of its finest fruits in this period. After the death of Charlemagne, his brilliant court circle declined and the center of cultural activity in the empire shifted to the monasteries. In these retreats work went on in the old pattern: Latin was studied, books copied, theological treatises composed, and history and biography written. Each monastery drew its membership from a wide territory and maintained constant contact with scholars in other monasteries throughout the west. The monasteries of the Frankish empire became refuges for a large number of scholars forced to flee from England and Ireland by the Viking attacks. These refugees brought with them precious books that enriched the monastic libraries and a range of talents that added depth and variety to intellectual and literary life. In the late ninth and early tenth centuries scholarly and literary activity shifted more into religious channels than had been the case during Charlemagne's day. Fundamental theological questions were discussed with insight and skill. Probably the most provocative theologian of the period was an Irishman, John Scotus Erigena, who wrestled with the problem of predestination and free will. Paschasius Radbertus composed an important work on the nature of the eucharist, which provoked a spirited quarrel among other theologians. The works of Agobard, Hincmar, and Jonas —all three important bishops—discussed problems in political theory concerning church-state relations and the nature of royal power. Histories and biographies, dealing in most instances with particular monastic houses and religious leaders, were produced. In spite of the increasing religious emphasis, however, there still remained a vital interest in the Latin classics. One of the most influential figures of the era was Rhabanus Maurus, a disciple of Alcuin, who carried on his master's interest in education and the liberal arts.

In these circumstances the church reasserted the domination of cultural life it had enjoyed prior to the Carolingian renaissance and again was able to stress those views and ideas that served its own interests. If the cultural achievements of the West in the ninth and early tenth centuries could not rival the brilliance of the Byzantine or Moslem worlds, they at least sustained a tradition of learning and a kind of education which, ultimately, were to provide the bases for Western Europe's reassertion of its cultural strength.

The picture of Western Europe in the last part of the ninth and the early tenth centuries would not, however, be complete without some mention of the effect of the political and social disorganization on the religious and cultural life of the period. The feudalization of lay society had powerful repercussions in the clerical organization of the times. High ecclesiastical offices were converted into fiefs and as a consequence often fell into the hands of ambitious secular nobles interested chiefly in their material exploitations. Church dignitaries holding feudalized offices were required to render all the obligations customary in the feudal system, including the basic duty of military service, and often found themselves slighting their spiritual functions in favor of secular affairs. Many tenth-century commentators on religious life complained that the secularization of the church hierarchy contributed to a decline in the spiritual life of the great mass of Christians in Western Europe. The civil wars and the barbarian invasions of the ninth and tenth centuries resulted in the destruction of many churches and monasteries, especially in England and northern France. The evolving feudal customs did not always nurture piety, social responsibility, and artistic or literary taste; in fact, the feudal noble of the age often had little respect for religious or cultural refinement. In this difficult phase Western Europe lacked the vigorous leadership it had enjoyed in the eighth and early ninth century, when Carolingian rulers, popes, and monastic leaders served as rallying points against the always present danger of a reversion to barbarism. This meant that the struggle to retain any degree of unity in the name of religion and culture had become desperate.

In the century after 850 each of the three great civilizations encircling the Mediterranean developed a degree of internal, primarily political, diversity not clearly evident before. Moslem and Western European civilization had been broken into several independent states, and in the West these were themselves divided into numerous feudal principalities. Byzantium had expanded her political strength so that she was able to draw into her orbit several Slavic kingdoms, thus creating a kind of community of states even though the Byzantine empire itself remained powerfully united. However, the emergence of diverse political units within the embrace of each civilization did not mean the end of the larger entity, the civilization itself. Religious and cultural forces still bound together the political fragments to the extent that each of the three— Western Europe, Byzantium, or Islam—was able to maintain the unique qualities around which their civilizations had been formed.

Conclusion ～～～～～～～～～～

HAVING traced the main events that marked the transition from classical civilization to the establishment of three new civilizations between the end of the sixth and the tenth centuries, let us conclude by again raising the question posed by Gregory the Great at the beginning of the period. What still remained of the delights of the world now that Rome was gone? A tenth-century observer, omniscient enough to comprehend the total picture in the lands once embraced by the classical way of life, could have supplied some answers.

He would have realized first of all that Gregory's age had been too pessimistic in concluding that classical civilization, symbolized by Rome, was gone. In the tenth century, traces of its influences were interwoven in the institutions, habits, and thoughts of men living in a vast area bounded by the Atlantic on the west and the Indus River on the east, by the North and Baltic seas on the north and the North African coastal region, Arabia, and Persia on the south. Churches and public buildings everywhere reflected classical styles in architecture and decoration. In classrooms, scholars' studies, and monasteries the works of Plato, Aristotle, Vergil, Horace, and other classical authors provided a major source of inspiration for philosophical, scientific, and literary studies. For statesmen and princes, Roman law was a guide for sound principles of statecraft. Perhaps most impressive of all to the tenth-century observer would have been the indications that the classical heritage had reached far beyond the limits of the Mediterranean world to affect Scandinavians, Bulgars, Moravians, and Russians, known barely or not at all by the classical Greeks and Romans. One of the great achievements of the post-Gregorian age was the successful effort of numerous different peoples to salvage significant elements of the dying classical civilization for their own use. In no small way these survivals contributed "things of delight" to the tenth-century world.

Our observer, however, would certainly have sensed that the tenth century possessed glories which did not depend on classical survivals. The great cities of the age would have offered decisive proof. Constantinople in the reign of Basil II was as impressive and vital as Periclean Athens or Hellenistic Alexandria or Augustan Rome. Its mighty walls, long an impenetrable barrier against hordes of enemies, symbolized the power contained within the empire ruled by the city. Its million citizens, ranging from the fabulously rich to the abjectly poor, lived exciting, purposeful, and secure lives within the framework of their own time and without undue longing for a superior classical age. The majestic, God-ordained emperor, living with his brilliant entourage in the magnificent Sacred Palace, loved and cared for his subjects. The great fleet in the harbor of the Golden Horn and the disciplined imperial guard stationed in the city kept danger at a distance. The countless shops and ateliers, supplied with raw materials from the whole civilized world and frequented by merchants eagerly seeking skillfully made products to sell abroad, provided ample opportunity to earn a livelihood. Thousands of priests and hundreds of beautiful churches provided spiritual sustenance. In the cloistered monasteries scattered through the city, monks prayed for the sinners and the afflicted, while in the great university learned men labored to increase their understanding of God's ways toward man. Relief from the ordinary routine of life was supplied by the races and athletic events at the Hippodrome and by the colorful processions that wound daily through the streets. Few cities in all history were richer in color and variety of life and setting than tenth-century Constantinople.

Much the same could be said for the chief cities of the Moslem world—Baghdad, Cordova, Cairo, and Damascus. Exquisite mosques and ornate palaces lent charm and beauty to each. The courts of their ruling princes were quite as dazzling and exciting. In their bazaars and shops the exotic products and peoples of the civilized world jostled one another in indescribable scenes of riotous color, sound, and motion. Characteristic of its more backward condition, Western Europe could claim no great capitals, with the possible exception of Rome, which was hardly cosmopolitan in the sense of Constantinople or Baghdad. It was chiefly a religious center, the site of the papacy and the great church of St. Peter, which drew numbers of pilgrims from all parts of Western Christendom. Their presence in the city, combined with the activities of the turbulent local aristocracy, provided a certain bustle and excitement, but nothing comparable to the Eastern cities. The West, largely cut off from the rest of the world by the difficulties and insecurities of travel, lacked the wealth, the trade, and the wide range of technical skills which brought people together in large numbers. Even Paris and London were only modest towns, dominated by feudal warriors or bishops. The fate of the capital of the Carolingian empire, Aachen, was typical of town life in the west. Instead of becoming a new Rome, as Charlemagne expected, it remained only a small community, strangled for lack of trade and industry and by the deepening political chaos.

Even outside the great cities of the tenth century there were signs that the world still had delights. Gregory the Great had complained that the fields he saw lay untilled, but one could hardly have maintained that complaint in the tenth century. The sturdy independent farmers of Byzantium, protected by the imperial government and their own essential contribution to imperial defense, enjoyed considerable prosperity. The rich farms of the Tigris-Euphrates and Nile valleys, where Moslem rulers had revitalized the irrigation systems, were never more productive. The rich grain fields and orchards of Spain were admired by all who passed. Across much of Western Europe the manorial system, by creating large estates tilled by peasant-serfs, had achieved a remarkable degree of self-sufficiency. It is true that productivity was not high on most manors, in part because the Western European economy offered no outlet for surplus produce, and there were still vast stretches of uncultivated lands interspersed among them. Nevertheless, within each manorial village there was a considerable degree of economic security and social stability, which combined to make the farmer's life tolerable and on some estates even prosperous. Benedictine monks were especially resourceful in creating new monastic estates and developing new agricultural techniques, particularly in those areas where they had come as missionaries. Thus on every hand there were signs that the end of the classical age had not meant complete impoverishment for the tillers of the soil and for those whose livelihood depended on agriculture. Between the sixth and the tenth centuries agricultural life had been reconstructed on a satisfactory basis.

Penetrating behind the externals of everyday existence, our observer would certainly have detected that the tenth century possessed its own spiritual, moral, and intellectual resources that likewise brought delight to the world. The religion of Mohammed, unknown to Gregory the Great, provided meaning and guidance in the lives of millions. Christianity itself had expanded its territorial sway, increased its authority, and enriched the lives of its faithful in the troubled centuries following Gregory's pontificate. In both Byzantium and the West its tenets supplied a guide and an inspiration for the revitalization of learning and education, and its concepts penetrated political institutions, social customs, family life, and morality to contribute direction and significance to the social order. In Byzantium the Christian organization was a powerful unifying force in support of the secular authority and a vital link between the empire and its satellites in the Slavic world. In Western Europe the international church headed by the pope furnished virtually the only unifying bond among the proliferating political units that had emerged. The beautiful liturgy celebrated in the great churches such as Hagia Sophia in Constantinople or St. Peter's in Rome, as well as in the tiny, crude chapels of Saxony, Bulgaria, Russia, or England, brought men closer to God and lifted up their spirits amidst the ever-present miseries of the world. The robust manners and customs of Germans, Arabs, Slavs, and Turks blended with the more sedate and civilized ways of classical society to invigorate the lives, enlarge the minds, and enrich the souls of the millions of heirs of classical civilization. In some cases these "new" people contributed substantially to the reconstruction of the political and social structure. Western European feudalism was powerfully affected by the practices of Germanic warlords, and prevailing legal systems were predominately Germanic. The brilliant poetry of the Abbasid period was colored by the ethos of the primitive Arab tribesmen.

All of these evidences of the material and spiritual accomplishments of the tenth century would have forced our observer to conclude that the end of the classical world had not been the end of all civilized worlds. The political institutions, the religious ideas and systems, the modes of thought and expression, and the economic and social organizations that were shaped during the early Middle Ages to replace the classical order provided a sound and satisfying base for the present lives and future dreams of men involved in each of these three civilizations.

True, the new modes of life were all different from the Graeco-Roman order, and each was distinct from the others. In this fact lay the key to an understanding of the early Middle Ages—those years so mistakenly referred to as the Dark Age. For the diversity that set the tenth-century world apart from the classical age and that distinguished Byzantine, Moslem, and Western European civilizations from each other was the consequence of creative effort expended in the centuries following 600. Mohammed, Charlemagne, Justinian, Benedict, Photius, Gregory the Great, and Harun-al-Rashid were pioneers. So were the Arab warriors, the Byzantine peasants, the Frankish nobles, the Benedictine monks, and the Western European serfs. They all had participated in the discovery and development of new ways of doing things, and in the process had reconstructed the bases of civilized life.

Our tenth-century observer could thus have answered without hesitation that there were many delights in the world. He might have wondered whether any of the civilizations he observed about him were as delightful as classical civilization had been. And he would undoubtedly have heard men about him arguing whether Byzantium, Islam, or the West provided the most pleasing, noble, or pious condition for mankind. But one thing was indisputable: civilization had not died with Rome; it had risen in new and different forms from Rome's ashes to launch mankind upon a new phase of history.

Chronological Summary

480–543　Career of Benedict of Nursia, founder of the Benedictine Order.

481–511　Reign of Clovis, founder of the Merovingian dynasty in the Kingdom of the Franks.

527–565　Reign of Emperor Justinian I.

c. 570–632　Life of Mohammed.

590–604　Pontificate of Gregory the Great.

610–641　Reign of Emperor Heraclius.

622　The Hegira, or emigration of Mohammed from Mecca.

634–713　Era of rapid Moslem expansion.

661–750　Umayyad dynasty rules Moslem Empire.

673–735　Life of Bede.

680　Sixth Ecumenical Council of Constantinople, settling the dispute over the nature of Christ.

711–713　Conquest of Spain by Moslems.

714–741　Charles Martel rules as mayor of the palace of the Franks.

717–741　Reign of Emperor Leo III the Isaurian.

717–718　Moslem siege of Constantinople fails.

726　Iconoclastic quarrel begins.

732　Battle of Tours; Franks check Moslem expansion.

735–804　Life of Alcuin.

741–768   Pepin the Short reigns as Frankish mayor of the palace and king.

750–1258   Abbasid dynasty rules Moslem Empire.

c. 750–1000   Golden Age of Moslem culture.

751   Pepin the Short elected first Carolingian king of the Franks.

755   "Donation of Pepin" establishes the papal states in Italy.

768–814   Reign of Charlemagne.

772–805   Charlemagne conquers and converts the Saxons.

774   Charlemagne conquers the Lombard kingdom in Italy.

c. 780–850   Carolingian renaissance.

780–850   Life of Al-Kwarizmi, Moslem mathematician.

786–809   Reign of Caliph Harun-al-Rashid, greatest Abbasid ruler.

796   Charlemagne destroys the Avar Empire.

800   Charlemagne crowned emperor by Pope Leo III.

c.   800   Viking raids begin to afflict Western Europe.

814–840   Reign of Emperor Louis the Pious; beginning of the decline of the Carolingian Empire.

843   Treaty of Verdun divides the Carolingian Empire.

843   End of the iconoclastic quarrel.

c.   850   Moslem Empire begins to disintegrate.

c.   850   Feudalization of Western Europe begins to develop rapidly.

858–867, 877–886

Patriarchate of Photius.

861   Conversion of the Moravians by Cyril and Methodius begins.

864   Conversion of the Bulgars begins by Byzantine missionaries.

865–925   Life of Al-Razi, Moslem medical authority.

867–1056	Macedonian dynasty rules Byzantine Empire; Golden Age of mediaeval Byzantium.
871–899	Reign of King Alfred the Great of England.
881–888	Reign of Charles the Fat, last Carolingian to rule the united empire.
893–927	Reign of Simeon, founder of the first Bulgarian Empire.
929	Foundation of a separate Moslem caliphate in Spain.
969	Foundation of the Fatimid caliphate in Egypt.
976–1025	Reign of Emperor Basil II.
980–1037	Life of Ibn Sina (Avicenna), Moslem medical authority and philosopher.
988 or 989	Conversion of Prince Vladimir of Russia to Christianity.

Suggestions for Further Reading

THERE are few good books in English supplying a synthetic treatment of the three civilizations in the early Middle Ages. Perhaps the best is H. St. L. B. Moss, *The Birth of the Middle Ages, 395–814* (Oxford, 1935). Also useful are Margaret Deanesly, *A History of Early Medieval Europe, 476 to 911* (London, 1956), and John L. LaMonte, *The World of the Middle Ages* (New York, 1949), although the former does not supply adequate information on Byzantine and Moslem history. Laborious but thorough are Vols. II–III of the *Cambridge Medieval History* (Cambridge, Eng., 1936), a co-operative work by several of the worlds leading scholars. For those who can use foreign languages there are several excellent books. Especially useful are Louis Halphen, *Les barbares des grandes invasions aux conquêtes turques du XIe siècle (Peuples et civilisations: Histoire générale*, ed. Louis Halphen and Philippe Sagnac, Vol. V; 5th ed., Paris, 1948); and *Das Mittelalter bis zum Ausgang der Staufer, 400–1250 (Propyläen Weltgeschichte*, Vol. III; Berlin, 1932).

Detailed histories of the Byzantine Empire are supplied by A. A. Vasiliev, *History of the Byzantine Empire, 324–1453* (2d Eng. ed., rev.; Madison, Wis., 1952), and George Ostrogorsky, *History of the Byzantine State* (Oxford, 1956; New Brunswick, N.J., 1957). These can be supplemented by J. B. Bury's monumental works, *History of the Later Roman Empire, 395–565* (2 vols.; London, 1923; Dover paperback, 1958), and *History of the Eastern Roman Empire, 802–867* (London, 1912). A shorter study which supplies a brief outline of Byzantine political history and a topical treatment of Byzantine institutions is J. M. Hussey, *The Byzantine World* (London, 1957). Also provocative are Norman H. Baynes, *The Byzantine Empire* (London, 1925), and Steven Runciman, *Byzantine Civilization* (London, 1933; Meridian Books, 1956).

Moslem history is well handled in Philip K. Hitti, *History of the Arabs from the Earliest Times to the Present* (6th ed.; London, 1956), and Carl Brockelmann, *History of the Islamic Peoples* (New York, 1947). Shorter but also sound is Bernard Lewis, *The Arabs in History* (London, 1950). The chief features of the Moslem religion are discussed concisely in H. A. R. Gibb, *Mohammedanism: An Historical Survey* (2d ed.; New York and London, 1953; New American Library, 1949), and A. Guillaume, *Islam* (2d ed., rev.; Harmondsworth, Eng., 1956; Penguin Books, 1954). There are many English translations of the Koran; especially recommended is that of N. J. Dawood (Penguin Books, 1957).

The problems of Western Europe in the early Middle Ages have prompted several provocative books in recent years. Especially interesting are Henri Pirenne, *Mahomet and Charlemagne* (London, 1939; Meridian Books, 1957); Christopher Dawson, *The Making of Europe* (New York, 1945; Meridian Books, 1956); C. Delisle Burns, *The First Europe. A Study of the Establishment of Medieval Christendom, A.D. 400–800* (New York, 1948); R. H. C. Davis, *A History of Medieval Europe from Constantine to St. Louis* (London, 1957); and J. M. Wallace-Hadrill, *The Barbarian West, 400–1000* (London, 1952). More topical in approach and more technical, yet extremely valuable for interpretations of the period, are Ferdinand Lot, *The End of the Ancient World and the Beginnings of the Middle Ages* (New York, 1931); Alfons Dopsch, *The Economic and Social Foundations of European Civilization* (New York, 1937); and William Carroll Bark, *Origins of*

the Medieval World (Stanford, Calif., 1958). A detailed study
of social and intellectual conditions during the troubled Merovingian era is found in Sir Samuel Dill, *Roman Society in Gaul
in the Merovingian Age* (London, 1926). Carolingian history
has never received an adequate treatment in English. The best
book on the Carolingian period is in French: Louis Halphen,
Charlemagne et l'empire carolingien (Paris, 1947). English history for this period is skillfully handled by F. M. Stenton,
Anglo-Saxon England (2d ed.; Oxford, 1947). The Vikings
are treated in Gabriel Turville-Petri, *The Heroic Age of
Scandinavia* (London, 1951). The complex problems of early
feudalism are treated with clarity in François Louis Ganshof,
Feudalism (New York, 1952).

Since ecclesiastical affairs loom so large in the history of
the early Middle Ages, church histories are invaluable for the
reader. Two books that are especially useful are Kenneth Scott
Latourette, *A History of Christianity* (New York, 1953), and
Philip Hughes, *A History of the Church*, Vol. I (2d ed.; New
York, 1949). Both emphasize the development of Christianity
in Western Europe but give some attention to Christianity in
Byzantium. They can be supplemented by Reginald Michael
French, *The Eastern Orthodox Church* (London, 1951). Full
of exciting suggestions about the role of the church as a civiliz-
ing agent in Western Europe is Gustav Schnürer, *Church and
Culture in the Middle Ages*, Vol. I (Patterson, N.J., 1956).
No serious student of church history can long avoid one of the
monuments of modern scholarship, *Histoire de l'église depuis
les origines jusqu'à nos jours*, ed. Augustin Fliche et Victor
Martin (Paris, 1934–); Vols. V–VII, written by several authorities, cover the period dealt with in this essay.

Helpful in the complex problem of cultural history is
Frederick B. Artz, *The Mind of the Middle Ages, A.D. 200–
1500* (2d ed.; New York, 1954), which supplies a broad outline of Western European, Byzantine, and Moslem cultural
activity. For Western European cultural history a sound work

is M. L. W. Laistner, *Thought and Letters in Western Europe, A.D. 500–900* (rev. ed.; Ithaca, N.Y., 1957). Also provocative is Henry Osborn Taylor, *The Mediaeval Mind*, Vol. I (4th ed.; New York, 1925). Although wider in scope than the period covered in this study, Norman H. Baynes and H. St. L. B. Moss, eds., *Byzantium. An Introduction to East Roman Civilization* (Oxford, 1948); Sir Thomas Arnold and Alfred Guillaume, eds., *The Legacy of Islam* (Oxford, 1931); and Gustave E. von Grunebaum, ed., *Medieval Islam. A Study in Cultural Orientation* (2d ed.; Chicago, 1953), are helpful in assessing the cultural role of the Byzantine and Moslem worlds.

A valuable book in placing the Slavs in the history of the era is F. Dvornik, *The Making of Central and Eastern Europe* (London, 1949). Especially good on early Russian history are George Vernadsky, *Ancient Russia* (New Haven, Conn., 1943), and George Vernadsky, *Kievan Russia* (New Haven, Conn., 1948).

Index